FROM THE REPORT OF THE 9/11 COMMISSION

"It is entirely plausible to suggest that [Jose Melendez-Perez's] actions in doing [his] job efficiently and competently may well have contributed to saving the Capitol or the White House, and all the people who were in those buildings, those monuments to our democracy, from being included in the catastrophe of 9/11, and for that we all owe [him] a debt of thanks and gratitude."

—Richard Ben-Veniste,
member of the 9/11 Commission

"Customs officer Jose Melendez-Perez stopped the 20th terrorist, who was supposed to be on Flight 93 that crashed in Pennsylvania. Probably because of the shorthanded muscle on that team, the passengers were able to overcome the terrorists. . . . He said, 'I don't care. This guy's a bad guy. I can see it in his eyes.' As he sent this guy back out of the United States, the guy turned around to him and said, 'I'll be back.' You know, he is back. He's in Guantanamo. We captured him in Afghanistan."

—John Lehman, member of the 9/11 Commission
and former Secretary of the Navy

"Every time he has been asked about his role in stopping the 20th hijacker, Mr. Melendez-Perez always says, 'I was just doing my job.' Well, Mr. Melendez-Perez, I say to you, 'Job well done.' "

—Ric Keller,
former United States Congressman from Florida

"[Jose Melendez-Perez is], without a doubt, a tremendous asset to CBP, an agency whose priority mission is to prevent terrorists and terrorist weapons from entering our country."

—*Robert Bonner,*
former Commissioner of U.S. Customs
and Border Protection

INSTINCT

ALSO BY THE AUTHOR

Flying Blind

Morning Drive

Murdered by Mumia

Muzzled: From T-Ball to Terrorism—True Stories That Should Be Fiction

INSTINCT

The Man Who Stopped the 20th Hijacker

MICHAEL A. SMERCONISH
with Kurt A. Schreyer

LYONS PRESS
Guilford, Connecticut
An imprint of Globe Pequot Press

Lyons Press is an imprint of Globe Pequot Press.

Text design: Sheryl P. Kober
Layout artist: Kim Burdick

Library of Congress Cataloging-in-Publication Data is available on file.

ISBN 978-1-59921-516-7

Printed in the United States of America

10 9 8 7 6 5 4 3 2 1

All author proceeds will be donated to the Flight 93 National Memorial.

TABLE OF CONTENTS

INTRODUCTION

Two thousand, nine hundred and seventy-three lives. The human toll of what the terrorists wreaked at the World Trade Center, Pentagon, and in Shanksville, Pennsylvania, is still mind-numbing. But it could have been even worse, much worse, except for the efforts—and perhaps more significantly, the instincts—of one man on one day, August 4, 2001. To the list of casualties sustained and landmarks vanquished we might well have added members of Congress and the Executive Branch, the nation's Capitol or White House. Indeed, in the course of "just doing his job," one man changed history and perhaps prevented the virtual decapitation of the United States government on September 11, 2001. His name is Jose Melendez-Perez.

On January 26, 2004, Richard Ben-Veniste of the National Commission on Terrorist Attacks Upon the United States— the 9/11 Commission—recognized Melendez-Perez:

> *Now, as we now know, with the benefit of investigations subsequent to 9/11, Mohamed Atta, perhaps the ringleader of all the terrorists here in the 9/11 plot, was at Orlando International Airport on August 4, 2001, the very day that Mohamed Kahtani claimed at least in part of his interview with you that someone was upstairs to meet him. And we know that Mohamed Atta made a telephone call from that location to a telephone number associated with the 9/11 plot. On the basis of that information, as well as significant additional information which we are not now at liberty to discuss in public session, it is extremely possible*

and perhaps probable that Mohamed al Kahtani was to be the twentieth hijacker.

Based on that premise, and taking into account that the only plane commandeered by four hijackers, rather than five, crashed before reaching its target, it is entirely plausible to suggest that your actions in doing your job efficiently and competently may well have contributed to saving the Capitol or the White House, and all the people who were in those buildings, those monuments to our democracy, from being included in the catastrophe of 9/11, and for that we all owe you a debt of thanks and gratitude.[1]

The audience in the hearing chamber of the Hart Senate Office Building erupted in applause. Commissioner John Lehman echoed those sentiments, calling Melendez-Perez a "first-class professional."[2] While speaking at the 130th Annual Meeting of the U.S. Naval Institute and Annapolis Naval History Symposium on March 31, 2004, Lehman added this:

One Customs Service officer stopped the 20th terrorist, at risk to his own career. Do you think he's been promoted? Not a chance. That is the culture we've allowed to develop. . . . Actions have consequences, and people must be held accountable. Customs officer Jose Melendez-Perez stopped the 20th terrorist, who was supposed to be on Flight 93 that crashed in Pennsylvania. Probably because of the shorthanded muscle on that team, the passengers were able to overcome the terrorists. Melendez-Perez did this at great personal risk, because his colleague told him, 'You can't do this. This guy is an Arab ethnic. You're racially profiling. You're going to get in real trouble, because it's against Department of Transportation policy to racially profile.' He said, 'I don't care. This guy's a bad guy. I can see it in his eyes.' As he sent this guy back out of the United States, the guy turned around to him and said, 'I'll be back.' You know, he is back. He's in Guantanamo. We captured him in Afghanistan. Do you think Melendez-Perez got a promotion? Do you think he got any recognition? Do you think he is doing any better than the 19 of his time-serving, unaccountable colleagues? Don't think any bit of it. We have no accountability, but we're going to restore it.[3]

Yet another 9/11 Commission member, Senator Bob Kerrey, was struck by "the kind of remarkable instincts" that Melendez-Perez showed at the border, and that he relied "on instinct alone to make sure that somebody who does have hostile intent against the United States of America is not getting through."[4]

Jose Melendez-Perez has much to teach us about using street smarts when it comes to protecting America, and he is not alone in that regard. Diana Dean was working as a Washington State border inspector when her gut told her something wasn't right about the man who would have been the Millennium Bomber. Michael Tuohey had a similar intuition when he looked Mohamed Atta in the eye on the morning of September 11, a suspicion no different than the staffer of a Minnesota flight school who alerted the FBI to the strange behavior of a new student named Zacarias Moussaoui.

This is their story.

CHAPTER ONE

A CHILLING EXPERIENCE

Shortly after 5:00 p.m. on August 4, 2001, a young Saudi arrived at Orlando International Airport on Virgin Atlantic Flight 15 from Gatwick Airport in London. His customs paperwork was for the most part blank. Because he apparently could not speak English, the primary immigration inspector could not communicate with him. Only the name was filled out on the required forms: Mohamed al-Kahtani.[1]

It would have been easy to regard him as just another befuddled tourist on his way to Walt Disney World. Unlike at Miami International Airport, where flights originating from countless overseas destinations arrive constantly, Orlando's foreign visitors are more intermittent and tend to fluctuate with the tourist season. Orlando International was then typically receiving one flight per day that originated in Saudi Arabia and had passed through John F. Kennedy International Airport in New York. British Air and Virgin Atlantic flights were noticeably more prevalent during the busy summer months. They arrived in Orlando daily from the U.K. and—prior to September 11, at least—did not raise many security concerns. Other foreign flights were considered more problematic in those days. Air Jamaica, for example, was receiving particular scrutiny from the government agency that was then known as the Immigration and Naturalization Service (INS). Flights from Brazil were also of concern because of a problem with fraudulent documents, while those from Santo

1

Domingo were known to carry passengers trying to immigrate to Puerto Rico.

In other words, the pre-9/11 mind-set had INS inspectors on the lookout for passengers who were visiting the United States with no intention to ever leave. Terrorism was not their most pressing concern.

Nothing about Kahtani raised eyebrows as he made his way into the United States. He had a visa that was less than a month old, but his passport documents appeared legitimate. As was the custom, however, immigration inspectors decided to run some computer checks on Kahtani's passport information. In advance of an airplane's arrival, INS inspectors were advised of the last overseas port of entry and the number of passengers aboard Virgin Atlantic Flight 15. They also used what was called the Advanced Passenger Information System (APIS) program. As soon as an airplane was in the air, the APIS manifest, complete with passengers' dates of birth, passport numbers, and countries in which they were issued, were made available to U.S. officials. The Passenger Analysis Unit (PAU) was then transmitted by the airline to INS, and staff would randomly check that list. Consequently, INS officials would have a range of information at their fingertips, including when a passenger bought the ticket, which agency purchased it, whether the traveler paid cash, when he or she checked-in, and whether that person was traveling with other companions.

On August 4, 2001, that computer process revealed nothing unusual regarding Mohamed al-Kahtani. That meant there was no indication that he was traveling with a false passport, or that the International Criminal Police Organization wanted him for criminal activity. Immigration inspectors almost always tried variations of a person's name and date of birth to guard against misspellings and other erroneously input data, and this procedure was followed in Kahtani's case as well. Still, nothing out of the ordinary registered. Nevertheless, because the man apparently could not speak English, standard protocol required that he be interviewed by a secondary inspector in order for INS to obtain the requisite information needed to complete standard paperwork—his arrival form (I-94) as well as his Customs Declaration. So at approximately 5:35 p.m. on this Saturday afternoon—when most people would be glancing at their watches in eagerness to leave work and go home—immigration inspector Jose Melendez-Perez walked to meet the newly arrived Saudi waiting in the secondary inspection area.

At the outset of his eight-hour shift, supervisor Edwin Bosch had assigned Melendez-Perez as one of three secondary inspection officers. It was a responsibility with which Melendez-Perez was familiar. As was the INS policy in Orlando at the time, inspectors customarily alternated between primary and secondary inspection stations. "The primary inspection inspector is the first official that an international traveler comes in contact with," Melendez-Perez explained in his testimony to the 9/11 Commission. "The officer's responsibility is to verify the passenger's travel documents for validity, the purpose of their trip, and to check entry/exit stamps for past travel history. In addition, inspectors query databases for passengers who may be on a lookout list for various reasons, such as terrorism, criminal records, outstanding arrest warrants, and so forth."[2] The databases available in 2001 included the Treasury Enforcement Communication System (TECS), a comprehensive clearinghouse that amasses a variety of information—physical descriptions and arrest records, for instance—on travelers entering and leaving the United States (it's accessed more than 700 million times a day);[3] the Central Index System (CIS–INS), which collects information on legal immigrants, naturalized citizens, and aliens already deported; and the National Automated Index Lookout System (NAILS), which contains information about individuals whose entry into the United States should be denied. Melendez-Perez had already earned a reputation as one who was conscientious in his duties and knowledgeable about the data and systems available to him. Then a fifty-five year old Army veteran who had served two tours in Vietnam, he had received a rating of "outstanding" in numerous categories of his annual evaluation as an immigration officer for several years running. More importantly, Melendez-Perez was highly experienced at interviewing and evaluating the many visitors—Saudis and others—to Orlando's famous tourist attractions. "My job requires me to know the difference between legitimate travelers to the U.S. and those who are not. This includes potential terrorists. We received terrorist and other types of alerts, such as document fraud and stolen passports, prior to September 11, but we all consider these alerts in a different light now,"[4] he testified to the 9/11 Commission.

Despite the 9/11 Commission's documentation of increased intelligence "chatter" in the summer of 2001, Melendez-Perez had received no reports of any heightened warnings during that time period. "Weekly, sometimes daily, we get information on documents that are being used to try to gain entry to the United States," he said. "Whenever there is a new type of document somebody is using, we are told. But beyond those normal reports, I remember nothing special about the months preceding 9/11. To be truthful, I had no awareness of al-Qaeda, or bin Laden before September

11th. If I did, it was only what I would have learned from television, not from my job."[5]

"If the Hell's Angels were due in town for Bike Week, we would have known about it, but not al-Qaeda,"[6] he said.

Melendez-Perez maintains a vivid recall of August 4, 2001. "My supervisor said something to me like, 'We have a guy who does not speak English and is a Saudi. Please take care of it.' So the first thing I did, even before seeing the guy, was to get his passport from the primary inspector, and enter it in the computer. I was looking to find any prior history of travel to the U.S., but in this case, there was nothing—the passport had no entries or stamps for the United States."[7] Not surprisingly, Kahtani's passport did contain stamps indicating that he'd traveled to a few Arab countries in the Middle East. Even with the aid of post-9/11 hindsight, however, there was nothing to indicate he had been to either Afghanistan or Pakistan for al-Qaeda training.

At the outset, Melendez-Perez had very little reason to suspect trouble from the man he was going to meet. In whatever was to follow, he would be drawing upon years of training—both before and after becoming an immigration inspector—and something he believes was given to him by God: instinct.

"Now it was time to go and get him in the waiting area," Melendez-Perez recalled of his first face-to-face encounter with Kahtani. "Picture me going into a room holding his passport with his photograph and looking around a room with about ten to fifteen people in it because other flights had just arrived. There he was at the end of the room, in the left corner." Describing Kahtani's appearance, Melendez-Perez said, "He was wearing a black long-sleeved shirt, black trousers, black shoes, black belt with silver belt buckle. He had no carry-on luggage. He had checked one bag, and it was on the carousel with everyone else's luggage." Above all, Melendez-Perez instantaneously registered the hateful arrogance in the man's eyes: "When I made eye contact, he immediately gave me a dirty look."[8]

The veteran INS inspector felt a cold chill run through his body.

CHAPTER TWO

LA GARITA

"Entre montañas y flores se encuentra también donde nací yo."

So begins a popular song about Jose's birthplace of Coamo, Puerto Rico—a treasure hidden "between the mountains and flowers" under a tropical sun. The song goes on to describe the exotic beauty of Coamo and its inhabitants. Though far away, the singer can never forget this enchanted, legendary place founded in the sixteenth century and commonly called "the old villa" since it was given that official title by Spanish royal decree in 1778. About fifty miles south of the capital of San Juan, Coamo is located in the lush green paradise of Puerto Rico's island interior.

Coamo's history is rich and diverse. Originally the third town founded by the Spanish on the island, it served as a regional capital until the late-nineteenth century. Yet its story is much older. Long before any Europeans arrived, Indians came to Coamo to bathe in the restorative waters of its many thermal springs. According to legend, it was the stories of these renowned hot springs that first inspired the famous Spanish conquistador Ponce de León, Puerto Rico's first governor, to search for the Fountain of Youth.

Today, time seems to have moved on as Coamo remains nestled snugly in the past. The architecture throughout the town still reflects Coamo's storied history. An inn and baths—Los Baños de Coamo—surround the famous springs and the complex was considered the island's most exclusive resort until the late 1950s. Far from the flashy modern casinos, hotels, and restaurants of San Juan and Ponce, Coamo's cozy shops, inviting cafes and open-air markets speak of its people's humility and nostalgia. In the center of town, an eighteenth-century church stands among the palm trees like an enormous white wedding cake.

Not all visitors to Coamo come to relax or shop. Every February, runners from around the world take up the challenge of its mountainous terrain in a hot, grueling 13.1-mile half-marathon. Besides tourism, the local economy is fed by manufacturing. Spurred on by tax incentives and duty-free access, U.S. firms like Westinghouse—which maintains a nearby plant—have been coming to Puerto Rico since the 1950s.

Born on January 2, 1946, Jose Melendez-Perez spent the first eighteen years of his life amid these beautifully exotic and multifaceted surroundings. His father, Nicolas Melendez, was born and raised in the town of Orocovis, home to many coffee plantations, as one of nine children—three girls and six boys. Jose remembers his father as a hard-working man. Nicolas owned *públicos*, or "public cars," which in Puerto Rico refer to independently owned and operated cars or vans that service difficult-to-reach areas. They resemble the limousine services of the United States, only the públicos that Nicolas Melendez drove were most often four-door sedans. He launched his business, which consisted of a few cars and drivers, in 1957, and passed away in 1998 at the age of eighty-six.

Jose's mother is Francisca Perez, and he honors her by taking the name Jose Melendez-Perez. She too was very industrious—working in a factory making women's nightwear while at the same time raising her children. Jose's parents were together for thirty years. Jose and his sister Betty, with whom he is very close, were born from that relationship. His other siblings—three brothers and three sisters—were from his father's other relationships. "Dad was a playboy," Jose says now, but a man who took responsibility for his offspring and instilled in them the value of working hard.[1] Jose's mother is now in her mid-80s and still resides in Coamo. So too does his younger sister, Ivette Margarita Melendez-Perez.

Melendez-Perez's formative years were spent attending school and helping his father with the family business. He washed cars every day. Sometimes he'd get up at three in the morning to wash cars before heading to school three hours later. In ninth grade, Melendez-Perez left school and worked as a furniture delivery driver for a department store, Valdejuly Segarra, while continuing to help his father eke out a living. For a flat fee of $2 one-way, passengers—mostly students at the University of Puerto Rico and workers from San Juan who lacked their own transportation—could ride in one of Nicolas Melendez's públicos. Nicolas would often transport up to six people at a time to make his business profitable enough to raise his children. If you were to ride in a público even today, you would probably find yourself sharing the ride with a family journeying to see a relative on the other side of the island. It's a tough way to make a living, and Nicolas's business was a one-man operation. "My father was no trouble. He worked hard. He was respected. People in our hometown loved and admired him. If he had passengers who needed to go to the university in San Juan, he would let them build up credit, sometimes up to $100, even if in the end he knew he would not get paid," Jose said.[2]

As close as he was to his family, Melendez-Perez left
Puerto Rico seeking a better life. In May of 1964, at the age
of eighteen, he joined the U.S. Army at Fort Gordon, Georgia. What attracted him to the military? Perhaps in part it
was the fond memories of journeys with his father to Fort
Buchanan, Puerto Rico. Jose remembers his father taking
him along on trips to the U.S. Army base, which is located
in the heart of the San Juan metropolitan area. Those were
the days before the toll roads of the late 1970s were built.
Route 14 was not a straight line. It was a three-and-a-half-
hour journey on a curvy, old road that traced its way up and
down the mountains and hillsides. Fort Buchanan, a hub for
the 15,000 U.S. reserve troops in Puerto Rico and the Virgin
Islands, is today the only Department of Defense location
in the Caribbean Basin area, according to the U.S. Army.[3]
But even when Melendez-Perez was a young man, the Army
base, like the ancient yet powerful architecture that guarded
the bay in the distance, symbolized only one thing: eternal
vigilance.

Due north of the base across San Juan Bay sits a more
ancient fortification. It is the sixteenth-century Spanish for-
tress of El Morro, famous for the *garitas*—or sentry boxes—
with which its massive battlements are studded. La Garita
has become, in fact, a national symbol of Puerto Rico and is
often depicted in travel guides and tourism promotions.

Melendez-Perez was sent to Fort Gordon in Georgia for
basic training. "I had just left Puerto Rico for the first time
and I can remember telling my father that I was thinking of
quitting during basic training, almost as soon as I began,"
Melendez-Perez said. "He told me that I had to stick it out.
He was very convincing that if I came home, I would come
home as a failure. He said to me, 'You must stick it out now,

because if you come back as a loser, you will lose integrity, and people will not trust you.' For that reason, I stayed."[4] Graduating from basic training, he then underwent advanced individual training at Fort Polk, Louisiana. Next, it was back to Fort Gordon for further advanced training followed by the elite U.S. Army Airborne School at Fort Benning, which is also located in Georgia. He was ultimately assigned to the famous 101st Airborne Division in Fort Campbell, Kentucky.

Melendez-Perez went to Vietnam in 1966 with the 173rd Airborne Brigade. The Sky Soldiers of the 173rd had been the first U.S. Army unit to be sent to Vietnam—they arrived in May of 1965—and would be the last to leave. As for most soldiers, his first tour lasted about a year. Melendez-Perez was subsequently reassigned to the 82nd Airborne Division. In 1970, he returned to the 173rd—and once again saw combat in Vietnam. Melendez-Perez served with distinction and was decorated for it. His commendations were destroyed when Hurricane Andrew devastated southern Florida in 1992, but he recalls receiving five Army Commendation Medals, which are awarded only to a soldier who "distinguished himself by heroism, meritorious achievement or meritorious service." Melendez-Perez was also awarded the Meritorious Service Medal on three occasions.

After coming home from Vietnam for the second time, he was assigned to Fort Dix in New Jersey as a basic training instructor. In the early 1970s, Melendez-Perez was forced to take a respite from his military service to assist his father with a personal crisis. But one year later, he returned to active duty, this time at Fort Benning, where he had once received his initiation into airborne warfare. Now, however, Melendez-Perez was assigned to the infantry school as a heavy weapons instructor.

The military is often (and unfortunately) quite adept at keeping its people moving from place to place, and this was certainly the case for Melendez-Perez. Between 1973 and 1976, he was assigned to a recruiting station located in the Bronx. Initially a recruiter, he also became a station commander and later an instructor during his time in New York City. Melendez-Perez was also an instructor at Fort Benjamin Harrison in Indiana. He served as a recruiter and station commander in Puerto Rico from 1976 until 1984, after transferring there to be closer to his family.

Melendez-Perez considers his years spent actively training and working as an Army recruiter to be crucial to learning methods of profiling, reading a person's body language, and sharpening his instincts of observation. "They taught me intense interviewing techniques," he said. "How to follow up with good questions. If you came to me at a recruiting station, I wanted to find out why you wanted to be in the military." He likes to use this analogy from civilian life: "Let's say you wanted to buy a car. I would ask, 'Well, what kind? What color, what make or model? Automatic or stick?' And on and on until I had exhausted every possible question about the car. And all along I would be listening intently to your answers and watching your body language, question after question after question. That is what I learned at the recruiting command."[5]

Melendez-Perez believes—and has proven—that basic principles such as these can be combined with immediate instinctive responses to bolster efforts to defend the country. He explained it this way: "It is the same thing today [as a customs and border protection inspector]. If I see a bad document, I ask, 'Where did you obtain it? From whom? Who introduced you to that person? How did you buy it?' And I keep going until I get everything I need."

The recruiting business isn't just about learning what a young person wants. Quite often the recruiter must glean information that is being withheld as well. While admitting that he was not "an interrogator of spies," Melendez-Perez nevertheless had to learn how to discover something that the interviewee would rather keep under wraps—like a criminal record. "I wanted to know if they had any previous arrests, especially in New York City. Out of every ten who said they wanted to join, it seemed like eight had a prior confrontation with the law. Many were minor, but you had to look into their eyes and decide if they were telling you the truth because if they fooled you, they would probably be found out at the processing station, but not until time and resources had been wasted on them."[6]

Melendez-Perez learned to read would-be soldiers very quickly—and he excelled at it. In 1977 and 1978, Jose was the top Army recruiter in the nation. In 1977, he was credited with 191 admissions, and in 1978, it was 202, which was unprecedented. Keep in mind that these were the years following the humiliating U.S. withdrawal from Southeast Asia, when the nation was engaging in some heavy navel-gazing about its foreign policies and—the Cold War not withstanding—the proper role of its military. The country was suffering from a moral and spiritual crisis often described as the "malaise" of the late 1970s.[7]

After twenty-six years of active duty and an Army life that kept him constantly on the move, Melendez-Perez decided to settle down. In 1994, he married his wife Carmen, who is also from Coamo. She brought to the marriage one adult son, Freddy. Jose has four additional children: Maribel, Brenda, Jose Jr. and Nelson. Maribel works in child welfare as an investigator in Puerto Rico. Brenda lives in Frankfurt, Germany, where her husband is an immigration and customs enforcement (ICE) officer serving at the U.S. Embassy in Frankfurt. Jose Jr. is a major in the U.S. Army who served in Afghanistan and was a commander in Iraq of the 319th Airborne Field Artillery Regiment of the 82nd Airborne Division. An Army ranger, he is currently a commander at the HALO (High Altitude, Low Opening) jump school. Nelson is a police officer with the Puerto Rico Police Department currently assigned to the Elite Fuerza de Choque Special Unit—the equivalent of a SWAT team here in the United States.

Melendez-Perez began his career with the Immigration and Naturalization Service in 1992 at the Federal Law Enforcement Training Center in Glynco, Georgia. Located along Interstate 95 about halfway between Savannah, Georgia, and Jacksonville, Florida, the Center is actually a small city that spans about 1,500 acres. According to the Department of Homeland Security, Glynco's facilities include everything from classrooms and dorms to firearms ranges (eighteen of them), an explosives range and a fully functional mock port of entry.[8] Jose spent sixteen weeks at the state-of-the-art training campus studying immigration law, weapons, defense tactics and criminal behavior and interrogation techniques.

Among other things, Jose says he "learned to follow a line of questioning, and watch for body language and body signals." He explains it like this: "For example, if a person goes to their embassy and obtains a visa and says they are coming to see Disney and stay for two weeks, then I would first ask them the purpose of their visit. That ought to be a very easy question to answer, but if they hesitate, then I need to keep pursuing a line of questioning." He continues: "If they are coming to stay illegally, quite often they choke, their response is not as spontaneous. They get nervous. In that case, I ask them if they are meeting somebody and how they will travel around. I am waiting to see how quickly they answer 'taxi' or whatever the case may be. At the same time, I am looking at their body language. When somebody is lying, the body gives me something. The lips may get dry, they may look to the ceiling, or they may look left and right. I am paying attention to everything. Most importantly, I try to be a good listener and good observer."[9]

"At Glynco, our training included hypothetical scenarios. Since September 11, there is new training. Today, they have more role-playing than before. That training alone is two weeks now," Jose says. "When I left INS training, I came home with two boxes of materials which were constantly being updated. Now, they also use a field inspector's guide."[10]

Melendez-Perez's first INS assignment was to Miami International Airport as an inspector. After two years he transferred to Orlando International Airport, where he remains today—now as a supervisor.

Prior to September 11, the INS was responsible for enforcing immigration law and managing the process by which individuals became U.S. citizens, while Customs handled all goods (meaning luggage and packages) entering the country. So on August 4, 2001—the day he encountered Mohamed al-Kahtani—Melendez-Perez was in the employ of INS, then a part of the Justice Department. Customs, however, was part of the Treasury Department. All of that changed with the creation of the Department of Homeland Security. As Robert C. Bonner, Commissioner of U.S. Customs and Border Protection (CBP), testified to the 9/11 Commission in January of 2004: "To create CBP, on March 1, we took most of U.S.

Customs and merged it with all of the immigration inspectors and border patrol from the former INS, and inspectors from the Department of Agriculture's Animal and Plant Health Inspection Service. This means that for the first time in our country's history, all agencies of the United States Government with significant border responsibilities have been unified into a single federal agency responsible for managing, controlling, and securing our nation's borders." The new agency became part of the Department of Homeland Security.[11] Now, CBP personnel like Melendez-Perez can be assigned either to passport control or baggage control. Once bearing the title of immigration inspector, Melendez-Perez is today a customs and border protection supervisor.

Was the change nominal—simply more bureaucratic paper shuffling?

"The national security element of my job [today] means that training and experience is important. In my case, training for my job as inspector has been threefold."[12] The first was his military service in Vietnam; Jose then brought his combat experience with him when he became an Army recruiter, which he calls the "second phase" of his preparation to be a CBP inspector. There he "learned effective listening skills, observation of body language, and determination of motives," he said.[13] The preparation and guidance he received at Glynco and subsequent "on-the-job" knowledge and skills acquired as an INS inspector form the third and final level of preparation that he would draw upon during his confrontation with Kahtani.

"I think one of the things that makes me good at what I do, and in life generally, is that since I was a kid, I take things very seriously, and I am very proud of what I do. I always give one hundred percent plus. That is my standard, that is my basic measure, and I always try to go beyond. Also, the value of integrity is one of the things I learned as a kid." He adds, "I am careful to do my job in the best way I can, to try to enjoy what I do, and to be proud of my effort."[14]

Melendez-Perez's instinct is, it seems, always on the job—sometimes to the annoyance of his wife Carmen. "My wife sometimes gets upset. If we go out to a restaurant, the first thing I do is look at everyone sitting there. 'Why is that guy over there doing that?' and so forth. I wonder to myself, Do they fit a profile of people you would expect to be eating here? Are they dressed the same way? Do they look out of place? And I always look for the exits."[15]

One night in 1994, Melendez-Perez was working in Orlando while staying in a small rented apartment. At about 11:30 p.m., he stopped to get milk. Two shady-looking individuals were also in the store, and Jose was convinced they were there to rob the place. After retrieving a jug of milk from the refrigerator, he calmly walked to the cashier and whispered, "Something is about to go down here." The cashier immediately alerted the police. The men fled.

By the time of that incident, Melendez-Perez had received years of INS training. He also brought to the situation a natural set of street smarts. Yet criminals, he acknowledged, can be conniving characters who are very adept at eluding an inspector's instincts and training. "I remember that one day a lady came to Orlando, a smuggler, and we denied her. She went to her embassy and complained, said she was just going to Disney and was improperly refused. Well, the next day, her boyfriend showed up, bringing a group of Japanese illegal aliens he was escorting—smuggling—into the U.S. We were ready for him because of her. I showed him a picture of his girlfriend and as soon as I did, he thought she'd turned him in. 'That f-----g b----!' he screamed. We busted him, too."[16]

So by the summer of 2001, Jose Melendez-Perez brought a wealth of training, experience, and natural ability with him as he walked into the secondary inspection room to question Mohamed al-Kahtani.

CHAPTER THREE

MALAFIDE

Mohamed al-Kahtani had only been waiting about fifteen minutes by the time he was first seen by Jose Melendez-Perez. So why the dirty look? "I said his name and asked that he follow me to a secondary inspection room," Melendez-Perez explained. As he did this, Melendez-Perez noted that the young Saudi gave him "a deep staring look." He testified to the 9/11 Commission: "Upon establishing eye contact, [Kahtani] exhibited body language and facial gestures that appeared arrogant."[1] The inspection room, one of six at Orlando International, is a ten-foot-by-ten-foot space with a desk, a computer, and a telephone. There are no windows to outside the building—just two panes of glass, but at the time they were covered by shades. "No one was watching," Melendez-Perez later explained, "although sometimes my supervisor would walk in. The discussion was not recorded. We sat opposite one another and the door remained open."[2]

Because Kahtani claimed he could not speak English, Melendez-Perez contacted the Justice Department to provide an interpreter. That day it was Dr. Shafik-Fouad, a Department of Justice employee officially certified in Arabic. With Kahtani seated across from him and Dr. Shafik-Fouad on the telephone, Melendez-Perez informed the translator that he had a man who had just arrived from Saudi Arabia via the U.K. and did not speak English.

The interview began. Dr. Shafik-Fouad translated: "I am Officer Jose Melendez-Perez of U.S. Immigration, and I am empowered to ask questions of you so that we may determine whether you are able to be admitted to the United States," Melendez-Perez stated.

"He just sat there and gave me a dirty look," Melendez-Perez recalled,[3] and in a split second, his mind registered the sneer and was telling him to observe closely and proceed carefully. As he testified to the 9/11 Commission: "Through my INS training and military experience, my first impression of the subject was that he was a young male, well groomed, with short hair, trimmed mustache, black long-sleeve shirt, black trousers, black shoes. He was about five-foot six, and in impeccable shape, with large shoulders and a thin waist. He had a military appearance."[4]

"You have just got to look at this guy's picture," Melendez-Perez would say later.[5] If Central Casting had been auditioning actors to play Middle Eastern terrorists that day, then a scowling Mohamed al-Kahtani would have gotten the role.

Through the interpreter, Melendez-Perez began his questioning. Having noticed that Kahtani did not have a return airline ticket or hotel reservations, his first question was, "Why don't you have a return ticket?" Upon hearing the question, Melendez-Perez later testified to the 9/11 Commission, "The subject became visibly upset and in an arrogant and threatening manner—which included pointing his finger in my face—he stated that he did not know where he was going when he departed the United States. What first came to mind at this point was that this subject was a hit man. When I was in the U.S. Army Recruiting Command, we received extensive training in questioning techniques. A hit man doesn't know where he is going because if he is caught, that way he doesn't have any information to bargain with."[6]

Just like the movies, Melendez-Perez, a huge fan of mafia films, thought to himself.

As the questioning continued, Melendez-Perez couldn't shake the impression that Kahtani had been trained in counter-interrogation techniques and had some military-like experience. For one thing, he was clearly unwilling to divulge the name of the person who was supposed to be meeting him at the Orlando airport. "He had no return ticket, did not know where he was going, and then said somebody else coming from overseas was supposed to make all arrangements for his transportation and where he was going," Melendez-Perez recalled.[7] He continued:

"I asked, 'Who is this person?'"

"He merely responded, 'A friend.'"[8]

As it turns out, Melendez-Perez's intuition that Kahtani had received military-like training in counter-interrogation tactics was exactly right. We now know this is a top priority among al-Qaeda training programs. An al-Qaeda instruction manual captured by police in Manchester, England, instructs its fanatical readers concerning "keeping secrets and concealing information." This secrecy should be used, the manual says, "even with the closest people, because deceiving the enemies is not easy."[9]

But, of course, Melendez-Perez did not have this manual or any other information about al-Qaeda available to him at the time. A seasoned interrogator, he nevertheless knew that Kahtani's evasiveness was indicative of possible criminal behavior. With his attempted concealments and arrogance, Kahtani may have thought that he was keeping information from U.S. authorities. But in fact his answers— and non-answers—were providing volumes of information. Jose's street smarts told him, "This guy does not know where he is living, why he is here, or where he is going next. A hit man does not know that sort of information." Looking back on the situation, Melendez-Perez feels his training taught him not only to ask the right questions, but to be sure to listen to the answers. He pressed Kahtani further about the "friend" whom he was supposed to be meeting. This, according to Melendez-Perez's sworn testimony to the 9/11 Commission, is the response that he received: "The subject then continued, stating that a friend of his was to arrive in the United States at a later date and that his friend knew where he was going. He also stated that his friend would make all the arrangements for the subject's departure. I asked him if he knew when his friend was to arrive in the United States, and he responded that he was to arrive in three or four days. I asked him what the purpose of this trip was and how long he wanted to stay. He responded that he would be vacationing and traveling through the United States for six days."[10]

Melendez-Perez quickly noted the problems with Kahtani's answers and realized that his story simply wasn't plausible. The 26-year-old traveler was hiding something. "Why would he be vacationing for only six days and spend half of his time waiting for his friend?" he thought. "It became apparent that the subject was being less than truthful concerning his true intentions."[11]

Melendez-Perez questioned him further, inquiring about where Kahtani intended to stay. He replied, "A hotel."[12]

Again unsatisfied with a brief, elusive answer, Melendez-Perez tried to encourage Kahtani to keep talking—despite the fact that Kahtani allegedly didn't speak English. (After all, he had been referred to secondary inspection because his customs declaration form and other paperwork were blank except for his name.) "I then told him that without knowledge of the English language or a hotel reservation he would have difficulty getting around Orlando. He answered that there was someone waiting for him upstairs."[13]

Now Kahtani's story had changed. In hindsight, it appears that he had cracked. In fact, we now know from testimony given in the Zacarias Moussaoui trial that Mohamed Atta—the hijacker flying American Airlines Flight 11 when it crashed into the North Tower—had indeed been expecting Kahtani. According to a written statement accepted as equivalent to Kahtani's testimony: "On August 4, 2001, Mohammed [sic] Atta drove to the Orlando Airport in a rented Mitsubishi Gallant . . . which he had rented on July 22, 2001, from Alamo Rent-A-Car. . . . While at the airport, Atta used a calling card . . . to call . . . the phone number for Mustafa al-Hawsawi," an al-Qaeda facilitator in Dubai. As it turns out, Kahtani "had the same telephone number for al-Hawsawi written on his airline travel documents."[14] It was this Dubai contact who, at the direction of Khalid Sheikh Mohammed, arranged Kahtani's travel to the United States and told him that he would be contacted there and given further instructions regarding a "martyrdom operation."[15]

In other words, Mohamed Atta was coming to pick up Kahtani according to the arrangements he had made with the al-Qaeda handler in Dubai. Documents recovered after 9/11 link both Atta and Kahtani to this same man, Mustafa al-Hawsawi. Of course, none of this was known to Jose Melendez-Perez. Nor had any INS inspectors, for that matter, been told by the CIA, the FBI, or any federal agency to look out for travelers from Dubai with contact information related to al-Hawsawi. Kahtani's paperwork listed al-Hawsawi's phone number in Dubai, but Melendez-Perez had not been provided the information on al-Qaeda that would have allowed him to make such connections.

When Kahtani mentioned that he was meeting someone at Orlando International Airport, Melendez-Perez pursued the matter. "When asked the person's name, he changed his story and said no one was meeting him. He said he was to call someone from his residence that would then contact someone locally to pick him up. I then asked the subject for the person's phone number and he refused to provide it stating that it was 'none of my business.' He stated that it was a personal matter and that he did not see any reason for me to contact that person."[16] As he said this, Kahtani was becoming increasingly hostile.

During the course of the ninety-minute interview, Melendez-Perez had to leave the secondary inspection room he shared with Kahtani three different times because, he said, the man's demeanor was quite literally chilling. "My feet were like two pieces of ice, and I was rubbing my arms and neck. I got some air and then I went back."[17]

Melendez-Perez didn't allow the growing antagonism to cloud his judgment. He recalled from the paperwork that Kahtani was in possession of $2,800 United States dollars and no credit cards. Considering this further, Melendez-Perez deduced that this amount would probably be insufficient for a six-day vacation plus a hotel room and return ticket. A one-way ticket to Dubai, where Kahtani had originated, would alone cost around $2,200. Melendez-Perez challenged Kahtani with this information in order to test his response. "When confronted with this fact, he responded that his friend was going to bring him some money," Kahtani recalled.

Melendez-Perez: "Why would he bring you some money?"
Kahtani: "Because he is a friend."
Melendez-Perez: "How long have you known this person?"
Kahtani: "Not too long."[18]

At that point, Melendez-Perez recalled, "I said to myself, 'I'd like to place him under oath.' I wanted him to understand the consequences of making a false statement. He agreed to be placed under oath, but when I asked the first question, he said, 'I won't answer.'" Now even the Arabic interpreter chimed in, "Something's not right here."[19] There was no way Melendez-Perez was going to allow this guy to enter the United States.

He left to inform his supervisor, Edwin Bosch, about the Kahtani case. Though he never directly questioned Kahtani, Bosch was supportive. The trust and back-up Bosch gave to Melendez-Perez was crucial because by then it was purely the INS inspector's instincts that were guiding him—they had no hard evidence to prove that Kahtani was a bad actor. While Melendez-Perez was interviewing Kahtani, another officer had checked his sole piece of luggage and had found nothing unusual or of interest. Melendez-Perez never examined the luggage, but it was reported to him that it contained just regular clothes. As he testified to the 9/11 Commission, "The subject's documents appeared to be genuine. A search of the subject and his personal belongings were also negative."[20] On the face of it, Kahtani might simply have been an irascible, jet-lagged tourist frustrated and angry that his inability to speak English was garnering him so much scrutiny. That was not, however, the opinion of Jose Melendez-Perez, and the veteran interrogator decided it was time to discuss the matter with his boss.

"At this point," Jose recalled to the 9/11 Commission, "I gave my supervisor a synopsis of the case and explained my suspicions that this individual was malafide (that is, his true intent in coming to the United States was not clear and he appeared very evasive)."[21] Bosch agreed that something was amiss, though any direct evidence was inconclusive. He decided that Juan C. Hernandez, the assistant area port director (AAPD), should be contacted for further instructions.

Normally, second-line supervisors like Hernandez are not called in for such matters, but because the INS had no specific grounds for removal of Kahtani, higher authorities would need to be consulted. Melendez-Perez recalls that Bosch telephoned Director Hernandez at home and explained Kahtani's strange behavior. He asked for his concurrence that the Saudi be denied entry into the United States and sent back to his place of origin. After hearing the facts in the case from Bosch, Director Hernandez then asked to speak directly with Melendez-Perez.[22]

In the meantime, a co-worker cautioned Melendez-Perez about second guessing a Saudi, because they were known to wield considerable political clout—and did not hesitate to use it when they believed they were being unnecessarily delayed. Those considerations failed to sway Melendez-Perez, who six days later would stop yet another Saudi who aroused suspicions upon arriving in Orlando. As Melendez-Perez explained to the 9/11 Commission, "Saudi nationals were held to the same legal standards as everyone else. However, servicewide they were treated with more 'tact.' For example, in order to accommodate the Saudi culture, female Saudis unwilling to unveil were inspected by female inspectors, if available. This remains the case today."[23] He added in an interview, "Many of the Saudis, the rich and famous, traveled with maids, drivers, and valets, and their documents were not so much of a worry. They were intimidating to many in the INS because if you delayed them, it could generate a congressional complaint. Many were very reluctant to offend the Saudis."[24] Bottom line: Admit a Saudi and you'll encounter no trouble. Question one—or worse, deny that person—and you risk the ire of a diplomat or politico, Melendez-Perez would later say. Yet when his co-worker warned him about starting trouble with a Saudi, Melendez-Perez responded: "I have to do my job, and I cannot do my work with dignity if I make my recommendations for refusals [or] admissions based solely on someone's nationality."[25]

Under what circumstances could the Customs and Border Protection (then Immigration and Naturalization Services) deny a person's entry into the United States? "In Orlando," Melendez-Perez would explain to the 9/11 Commission, "as in any other port, an Immigration inspector can only return someone foreign back home, for whatever reason, under the Expedited Removal law if the inspector is able to substantiate the recommendation. Supervisors for the most part support inspectors who have enough proof to substantiate removing someone. Nevertheless, it is my belief that some supervisors in Orlando and nationwide remain intimidated by complaints from the public, and particularly by congressional letters, when certain aliens are refused admission. Because of these complaints, supervisors tend to be wary of supporting the inspector who recommends an adverse action against an alien."[26] He would later add, "In order for a supervisor to back you up when you are going to deny someone admission, you had better have proof. Do you have a farewell letter from a girlfriend in the suitcase saying he is leaving? That would be proof he intends to stay."[27]

"Just being suspicious gets touchy because many supervisors don't want to make a decision. If you turn back the wrong person, you run the risk that the person goes to their embassy and before you know it, you get a congressional letter."[28] When asked if the situation has improved since September 11, Melendez-Perez responded, "I do not know how often people are removed from the United States, nor can I tell you, before 9/11, how many Saudis entered the country or how many were refused. However, I can tell you that according to the records we have in Orlando, approximately ten Saudi nationals have been turned around for various reasons."[29]

Well aware of the pressure to give Saudi visitors special treatment, Melendez-Perez picked up the phone and spoke directly with Director Hernandez. He remembers that Hernandez asked numerous questions concerning the case. "I explained that apart from not having a return ticket and possibly not having sufficient funds, [Kahtani] appeared to be a malafide."[30] Melendez-Perez wasn't afraid to report to Director Hernandez what his gut was telling him, and the director responded by listening with great interest and concern. As Melendez-Perez later recounted to the 9/11 Commission, "I further explained to the AAPD that when the subject looked at me, I felt a bone-chilling cold effect. The bottom line is, 'He gave me the creeps.' You just had to be present to understand what I am trying to explain."[31]

After listening carefully to Melendez-Perez, Director Hernandez suggested that "under Section 235.1(a)(5) of the Immigration Nationality Act an applicant could be required to state, under oath, any information sought by an Immigration Officer regarding the purpose and intentions of the applicant in seeking admission to the United States."[32]

As Melendez-Perez later told the 9/11 Commission, Director Hernandez "was convinced from what I had stated and my beliefs about the subject that the individual was in fact a malafide and should be allowed to withdraw his application or be set up for Expedited Removal."[33]

During his interview of Mohamed al-Kahtani, Melendez-Perez took note of the Saudi's begrudging responses and other information that he then used to fill out what's known as the I-275, the Withdrawal of Application for Admission. This standardized form requires the immigration inspector to fill in the person's name, citizenship, address, flight, day of arrival, visa type, and so forth. A blank space is also provided for the officer to record what had happened. Melendez-Perez not only filled in the blank, he attached a full page of narrative. Melendez-Perez also completed a second form, known as an I-213, or Record of Deportable/Inadmissible Alien. There is more information on the 275 than the 213, but one item not provided by the former is the subject's occupation. Kahtani said he was a car salesman. Altogether, the universe of Kahtani's paperwork included: the I-94, custom declaration, I-275, I-213, passport, visa, plane ticket, system check, and IDENT enrollment—including a photo and fingerprints taken on an FD-249 (red) form, which later proved highly valuable in the eventual capture, identification and detention of Kahtani.

Having the support of his supervisor as well as the assistant area port director, Melendez-Perez returned to the secondary screening room where he had left Kahtani. His 9/11 Commission testimony explains what happened next: "I then proceeded to advise the subject that he did not appear to be admissible to the United States. He was offered the opportunity to voluntarily withdraw his application for admission."[34] Fuming, Kahtani refused to pay for his flight home. Melendez-Perez informed the Saudi that if he was unwilling to pay his own way, then he would be detained by U.S. authorities until the matter was resolved. Kahtani then decided to pay his own way rather than wait. He chose to withdraw, signed the I-275, and was escorted to his departing gate by Melendez-Perez and another immigration inspector, Melendez-Perez later testified.[35] Melendez-Perez also saw to it that the documentation regarding Kahtani's denial of admission was being provided to British authorities so they would know that they had a bad actor headed their way.

The inspection process being implemented was following a succession of steps. The individual in question was interviewed to determine the nature of the problem. Next, the secondary inspector—Melendez-Perez—needed to establish grounds for the visitor's inadmissibility with his or her supervisor. Then, the visitor was placed under oath in order to formally document the facts that had been uncovered during the screening process. Finally, the foreign visitor was offered a choice: either to withdraw the request for admission to the United States or be forcefully expelled.

Kahtani did one more thing that gave Melendez-Perez chills—something that the inspector immediately recalled upon hearing of the attacks on the World Trade Center and Pentagon the following month. Kahtani was about to board Virgin Atlantic Flight 16 to London with a connecting flight to Dubai. As Melendez-Perez later testified, "Before boarding the aircraft, the subject turned to the other inspector and myself and said—in English—something to the effect of, 'I'll be back.'"[36]

A postscript to this interaction later came from none other than Khalid Sheikh Mohammed, the bin Laden deputy appointed to mastermind the September 11 attacks. After his capture, Sheikh Mohammed would tell his investigators of his frustration and disgust with Kahtani. He was "too much of an unsophisticated 'bedouin' to function with ease in a modern, Western society," KSM reported. Yet he knew as well that Kahtani was not entirely to blame. Al-Hawsawi, the al-Qaeda logistician in Dubai who was responsible for sending Kahtani off to the United States, had left clues about the real purpose of his visit. Sheikh Mohammed grudgingly complained that the Dubai facilitator gave Kahtani "only a one-way ticket and provided him with only limited information about his points of contact in the U.S."[37]

Of course, the computers, the documentation, and his co-workers all told Jose Melendez-Perez that everything about Mohamed al-Kahtani ought to be business as usual. Nevertheless, a major battle in the war on terror was fought on August 4, 2001, and the United States won. Nobody knew it yet.

"Are you crazy, two Saudis in less than a week? This will get you in trouble!" These were the words aimed at Jose Melendez-Perez by a fellow immigration inspector at Orlando International Airport when, six days after denying Mohamed al-Kahtani permission to enter the United States, he now found himself refusing to admit another supposed tourist from Saudi Arabia.[38]

The man—whose name was also Mohamed—arrived on a Saudi Arabia Airline flight direct from Jeddah, Saudi Arabia. Jeddah, which lies on the shores of the Red Sea, is the closest major city to the holy city of Mecca. For that reason, the city has been a popular stopping point for Muslim pilgrims making a *hajj* since the seventh century. The traveler leaving Jeddah on August 10, however, appeared to Melendez-Perez to have less than pious intentions. Arriving in Orlando, this Saudi presented himself to the primary immigration inspector as a tourist who simply wished to visit the United States for pleasure and recreation. He presented a valid passport with a valid visa, and—unlike Mohamed al-Kahtani—he had correctly filled out an I-94 arrival & departure form, which included the address of a friend with whom he said he intended to stay during his monthlong vacation. The only problem—and one that led this second Saudi named Mohamed to be flagged for secondary inspection—was that he had no return ticket, only fifty U.S. dollars in cash, and no credit card.

Melendez-Perez was again assigned to secondary inspection on that day. During the interview, the Saudi claimed that a friend was going to purchase a return ticket because he owed Mohamed a thousand dollars from the friend's last trip to Jeddah. The man also stated that his friend was waiting for him upstairs at the international arrival area of Orlando International Airport. Melendez-Perez decided to check the guy's story out, so he called the Saudi Arabia Airlines desk at Orlando and asked them to find the friend. He could not be found.

When told that his friend could not be located upstairs, the Saudi visitor then provided a telephone number—only it was prefaced with an unusual area code: 402, the code for Lincoln, Nebraska. Perplexed, Melendez-Perez called the number. A man answering by the name the Saudi supplied spoke with Melendez-Perez, but the story he told did not match what had been said by the man seeking admittance to the United States. Instead, the individual who answered the call said he was in Lincoln, not Orlando. And while he said he knew the man now in front of Melendez-Perez, he further explained that Mohamed's mother had called him only the day before (August 9) to inform him that her son was inbound to the U.S. from Saudi Arabia aboard Flight 55 from Jeddah to Orlando via JFK Airport. The man on the phone told Melendez-Perez he was not going to be in Orlando for two to three days because he had to drive there. The Saudi was apparently expected to wait for him at the airport.

Melendez-Perez recalls his response to the man in Nebraska: "I explained that it was impossible—that it was not proper for us to admit a passenger without sufficient funds and no return ticket. I also explained that the subject cannot stay in the airport without enough money—for two days—without any guarantee that he will be met."[39] The man replied that he would call him back. Upon learning of that response, Mohamed, the newly arrived Saudi, provided Melendez-Perez the number of yet another friend— this one with a Tampa, Florida, area code—not exactly close to Orlando, but better than Nebraska. Mohamed handed Melendez-Perez the number along with a story saying that he had stayed with this friend in Tampa for two weeks on his last visit, which had been about a month before. Seeming to support this story, Melendez-Perez noted, was the fact that Mohamed was in possession of a Florida ID with this Tampa man's address. Melendez-Perez dialed this man's number. Like the Nebraska contact, the Tampa man said he knew Mohamed but had not seen him in a long time. He also stated that he was busy working and had no time to come pick Mohamed up. For the second time in less than a week, Melendez-Perez had a gut feeling that something wasn't right. He remembers asking the Tampa man "You haven't seen him in a long time? He just departed, you know, thirty days ago." The man then responded "that he didn't have time to talk to me or take care of [Mohamed]." "This guy sounded like he didn't want any contact with Mohamed," Melendez-Perez recalled.[40]

Rather than wind up with a stranded traveler who'd been inconsistent and flighty during his screening interview, Melendez-Perez called Nebraska again to see if the man there would make a hotel reservation for Mohamed or an airline reservation to Lincoln. "After waiting for three hours, I could not get him to agree on any of the requests."[41] Melendez-Perez was left with no other option but to deny admission based on immigration rules. Consequently, the Saudi was allowed to withdraw his application for admission. As part of this procedure, Melendez-Perez then questioned Mohamed under oath in order to obtain a sworn statement. In doing so, he asked the visitor if he had any family in the United States. Mohamed rather surprisingly responded yes, an uncle living in Texas, but could offer no address or telephone number. When asked again when he last visited this country, Mohamed gave another surprising answer: he responded that he arrived at JFK on March 23 and stayed for two weeks. This statement directly conflicted with his previous tale about visiting Tampa only a month or so before. The contradictory account only reaffirmed Melendez-Perez's decision to deny entry to this mysterious man who couldn't keep his story straight.

Though the Saudi was clearly more familiar (and almost at home) with American culture and behavior, there was something exceedingly wrong about him. Though he did not give Melendez-Perez an alarming "chill" in the way that Kahtani had just a few days before, the man's reluctant "friends" in America who were not too eager to see him, and his misleading statements about previously visiting the United States, aroused Melendez-Perez's suspicion. The man subsequently departed the United States the next day—August 11, 2001, aboard a Saudi Arabia Airlines flight from Washington D.C. Melendez-Perez has no further information to make a firm connection between this incident and the one involving Kahtani on August 4. As Melendez-Perez now explains, "I did think about it. But to be honest, I didn't think about it that hard, because remember, that [post-9/11] mentality wasn't there. But I knew that something wasn't right [about the events of August 10.]"[42]

"This guy was calm and collected . . . like he'd been here before and thought that he had all the angles covered,"[43] Melendez-Perez recalled. After September 11, he did make the connection and notified federal authorities. Melendez-Perez wonders if the second Mohamed was possibly sent by al-Qaeda as a replacement for Kahtani. After all, he thought, this second man had traveled to and from the United States before, possibly working here for an extended time. If al-Qaeda wanted to replace Kahtani, then this guy would make a good candidate—particularly on short notice.

Eight years removed from September 11, 2001, Melendez-Perez remains unsure of the status of the FBI's investigation of the second Saudi visitor as well as the man's whereabouts since being prevented from entering the U.S. "The only thing that I can tell you is that . . . some time ago . . . I received a call from an FBI agent. They wanted a copy of this guy's picture if we had one. And the reason that they wanted this information was that they found a passport somewhere, in a raid that they did, and it seems like they thought that one of the passports that they encountered belonged to that person."

"They said they were investigating, and that they would get back to me in the future," Melendez-Perez later said.[44]

He never heard back.

CHAPTER FOUR

INSTINCT

FLAT BLACK EYES

Malcolm Gladwell, author of the best-selling book *Blink: The Power of Thinking Without Thinking*, suggests there is value in "rapid cognition." Gladwell explained that the book "is concerned with the smallest components of our everyday lives—with the content and origin of those instantaneous impressions and conclusions that bubble up whenever we meet a new person, or confront a complex situation, or have to make a decision under conditions of stress." He added: "I think its time we paid more attention to those fleeting moments. I think that if we did, it would change the way wars are fought, the kind of products we see on the shelves, the kinds of movies that get made, the way police officers are trained, the way couples are counseled, the way job interviews are conducted and on and on."[1]

That is not to say that our instincts are foolproof. Rapid cognition can often go awry, Gladwell noted: "For some reason corporations overwhelmingly choose tall people for leadership roles. I think that's an example of bad rapid cognition: There is something going on in the first few seconds of meeting a tall person which makes us predisposed toward thinking of that person as an effective leader, the same way that the police looked at my hair and decided I resembled a criminal."[2]

Well, rapid cognition worked for Jose Melendez-Perez. But he is not alone. Ask any cop about the value of street smarts and intuition. Or consider the work of Diana Dean.

Something didn't seem quite right to the twenty-year veteran customs inspector about the green Chrysler 300M with Quebec tags that pulled up at about 6:00 p.m. on the evening of December 14, 1999, in Port Angeles, Washington. The first thing Dean noticed was that the car was very nice— almost too nice to be arriving late on a Tuesday in this small town of eighteen thousand near Vancouver, British Columbia. She then observed that the driver was a lone male. And something about him and the circumstances of his arrival didn't fit the pattern of travelers she'd come to know in the ten years she had worked at Port Angeles. Nothing nefarious crossed her mind, but the situation was, in her words, "interesting"—and she definitely wanted to ask him a few questions.[3]

The driver said his name was Benny Norris, but his real name was Ahmed Ressam, a thirty-three-year-old Algerian who, along with other Islamic radicals in a Canadian al-Qaeda cell, was attempting to pull off what authorities would later call a foiled 1999 "millennium bomb plot." Ressam's target was to be the Los Angeles International Airport.[4]

There were no terrorist watch lists being distributed to U.S. border inspectors at that time, and no information database could have tipped off Dean to Ressam's activities. Her curiosity piqued by this eccentric visitor, she began asking him a few questions. Inquiring about his destination, Dean noted the man's French accent, which complied with the tags on the car. Still, he was a long way from home. Learning that he was headed to Seattle, she asked the question familiar to anybody who has traveled outside of the United States:

"What is the purpose of your visit?" Dean noticed that the man seemed a bit nervous, almost "squirming a bit" when she asked him the question.[5] "Business," he replied.

"Where do you live?" she asked. An easy question, perhaps, but by this point Dean was paying attention to more than what the man was saying. Why was he only giving one-word responses to her questions when he obviously understood what she was saying? The answers were appropriate, but they were also brief and guarded. The man was acting "hinky," she would later say.[6] There was really no other way Dean could describe what her instincts were telling her. Why was he fidgeting around with the driver's console? He mumbled something about his itinerary, but he wasn't making sense. Was he looking for a gun? Why would a tourist here for a simple "visit" be so jittery? And why was he sweating?

"His story didn't make sense to me," the now-retired Dean said.[7] "The driver had detoured hours out of his way to make the ferry" for what was ostensibly a trip to Seattle.[8] That struck Dean as odd because Port Angeles, a sleepy little town that faces the scenic Olympic Mountains on one side and the Pacific Ocean on the other, is an ideal getaway destination, but hardly on the way to the state's largest city. The town is located along the northern edge of the Olympic Peninsula in Washington State, about seventeen miles directly across the Strait of Juan de Fuca from Victoria, British Columbia. But it's ninety miles to Seattle, and if someone from Canada was headed there, they would be expected to take Interstate 5 or some other route far to the East. People come to this far-off corner of the country to escape—not to encounter—the hustle and bustle of big city life, and they find plenty of climbing, hiking, kayaking, mountain biking, sailing, skiing, surfing, and scuba diving to distract them from the rat race back in Seattle, Portland, or the Silicon Valley.

Remaining calm but alert, Dean asked the man whom he was going to visit in Seattle. "Hotel" was the response.

Another one-word reply. Dean needed to know more, and she wasn't getting it from this strange visitor. She was certain that the car needed to be searched. She instructed him to turn his engine off and fill out a customs declaration form, which he did. As he was filling out the form, Dean tried to chitchat with Ressam, but he wasn't responding. Unable to speak French, she decided to ask colleague Mark Johnson, who had worked for a while in Montreal, to talk to Ressam. Johnson didn't speak French either, but Dean hoped he might nonetheless be able to get the stranger to open up. Dean wondered if, because she was a woman, perhaps she was making the foreigner uncomfortable or simply just not "getting him." Johnson, she thought, might somehow be better equipped to communicate with the visitor.

But Johnson's attempt was unsuccessful as well. Remaining amicable with Ressam, Dean politely asked him to step out of the car and open the trunk "so we can take a quick look and get you on your way." But the man was hesitant, and they had to open his door for him. Fortunately, another inspector, Carmon "Dan" Clem, had finished his work and came over to help out. There were now three of them with Ressam.[9]

Ressam was wearing a long, camel hair coat that looked to Dean "five sizes too big for him." While she stayed to inspect the vehicle, Johnson took Ressam aside to do a pocket check. The interior of the car itself was unremarkable. In the trunk they found one small suitcase, which they removed and examined. Meanwhile, Inspector Clem, following standard procedure, checked the wheel well. "Um, Diana," he said. The tone of his voice alerted Dean to come and take a look. Looking into the trunk, Dean saw several large plastic bags containing an unknown substance. Thinking that they may have uncovered a drug stash, she went inside to call for backup. It all seemed to fit: the expensive car and coat, the suspect's reluctance to answer questions, and his choice of the tiny town of Port Angeles as his border crossing point. As Dean left to make the necessary phone calls, Inspectors Johnson and Clem brought Ressam over to the car. A large man, Johnson wisely kept his hands on Ressam's shoulders as he escorted him back to take a look. As Johnson recalls, he could feel Ressam shudder when he saw what the inspectors had found. Seeing the bags, Johnson decided to give the man another pat-down to look for weapons. At this point, Ressam slipped out of the oversized coat that he was wearing and took off down the street in a desperate attempt to escape.[10]

Hearing the commotion outside, Dean ran out of the office with another inspector who had been filling out paperwork in time to see Johnson, Clem, and a third inspector, who had been examining the contents of the suitcase, all running down the street after Ressam. One of them yelled back to them to get a car. Dean remained to guard Ressam's car while the others went in pursuit. In less than ten minutes, she saw a police patrol car return with Ressam handcuffed in the back seat. He had gotten about four blocks away. When he tried to steal a car that was stopped at a red light, the driver had the presence of mind to lock her doors and hit the gas through the intersection. This slowed Ressam long enough for the inspectors to catch up with him.[11]

As all of this was unfolding, Dean and the other customs inspectors were assuming that Ressam was a drug runner. That last thing on their minds was that the mysterious contents of those black plastic bags in the trunk were bomb-making materials. On the other side of the border, however, authorities knew who Ressam was and had strong suspicions about what he was up to. For months Ressam and other members of his Montreal cell had been under the surveillance of the Canadian Security Intelligence Service (CSIS), which had been tipped off to the presence of an al-Qaeda recruiter by the famous French inspector Jean-Louis Bruguière. Bruguière was, according to a subsequent *Seattle Times* report, "the world's most prominent terrorist tracker," the man responsible for pursuing the French Action Directe, a group associated with many bombings in the 1980s. He had tracked and located Carlos the Jackal, the Venezuelan-born terrorist implicated in several European attacks.[12] And yet he was powerless to do anything—as were Italian agents who were also concerned about this Montreal cell and had also warned the Canadian authorities.[13] Facing a forbidding legal terrain similar to "the wall" encountered by the CIA during the 1990s, the CSIS had its hands tied. "Its mission did not include chasing down ragtag thieves and immigration violators," the *Seattle Times* reported.[14] Fortunately, for all of his terrorist training in Afghanistan (not to mention his prior experience as a thief), Ressam's nerves were apparently not up to the job when it came to crossing the border with his bomb.

With Ressam in custody, the customs inspectors at Port Angeles began testing the substance in one of the larger bags for every possible drug they could with the test kit they had available. Nothing. Why, then, did the man run from authorities? The inspectors decided to take a closer look at the car, and when they did so, they found electrical boxes, wires, and strangest of all, an olive jar containing a honey-like substance with wood chips suspended in it. Opening one of the four electrical boxes, Inspector Johnson noticed a wrist watch. "What do you make of this?" he said to Dean's husband, a retired customs inspector now on the scene. It began to dawn on them that they weren't dealing with a drug runner at all. They had apprehended a would-be bomber.[15]

"F-----g S--t!" Dean's husband exclaimed. Dean herself said she still breaks into a cold sweat when she tells this part of the story. Her heart, she continued, sank to her toes, and she felt like a zombie as she walked outside to the car to inform the police officer just what kind of perpetrator they had in custody. Looking straight at a patrolman on the scene, she heard herself say, "This guy is a friggin' terrorist." They stared at each other for what seemed like hours. What exactly was the substance in those bags? Could the car blow up at any moment and take the entire pier—and them—with it? And who was Benny Norris, aka Ahmed Ressam, really?[16]

Dean immediately telephoned the port director, as well as the FBI office in Seattle and the regional office of the Bureau of Alcohol, Tobacco, Firearms and Explosives (ATF). Their initial skepticism was understandable. The inspectors in Port Angeles were still coming to grips with the situation. As Dean would later say, "It was 1999, so it was a little difficult to get people to believe what you have. They're not there. They don't see it. By this time it was 7:00 at night, and so their reaction was 'Come on—you want us to do what? You want us to come to Port Angeles out in the middle of nowhere?' "[17] Once the details of Ressam's arrest were explained, however, the federal law enforcement agencies knew that this was no minor drug bust. This was something serious, and they would need to investigate it. Before she knew it, Dean's tiny trailer, which customs inspectors at Port Angeles used as their main office, was jammed with representatives from the FBI, ATF, Immigration, Border Patrol, Coast Guard, Washington State Patrol, and local police.

In many respects, Dean said, "we were all in uncharted waters."[18] The initial tests performed by ATF agents on the mysterious substances found in Ressam's vehicle were inconclusive. Even if the materials could be assembled together to make a bomb, they technically couldn't point to something and say: "That's the bomb he tried to smuggle across the border." So what were they to charge him with? Agents did find several driver's licenses in the car, however, and the different aliases on them confirmed that Ressam wasn't who he presented himself to be. He wasn't saying anything. Immigration was able to charge him while the FBI continued its investigation.[19]

Dean later testified to the U.S. Senate Judiciary Committee: "Further examination of Ressam's vehicle resulted in the discovery of four timing devices and a total of 118 pounds of urea crystals, 14 pounds of sulfate powder, and 48 ounces of nitro-glycerin."[20]

When Jose Melendez-Perez first locked eyes with Mohamed al-Kahtani in the secondary inspection area of the Orlando International Airport, he experienced an overwhelming feeling, an icy chill that told him he was dealing with a dangerous individual. Diana Dean says she had a similar feeling in the presence of Ressam. Clearly there was also something amiss about him when he drove up to Dean's inspection station at Port Angeles. There was something that just didn't fit, but she became particularly concerned about Ressam when they brought him, handcuffed, from the patrol car into the customs inspection trailer. "I looked at him," she recalled, "and when I looked at his eyes—you know how when you look in someone's eyes you see a light? There's somebody home there. His eyes were flat black, just like they were dead. There was no personality, there was no life, there was nothing in his eyes. To look at them made my blood run cold. I mean, I knew that this is very bad."[21] According to Dean, the mug shot of Ressam seen nationwide following his arrest was taken at the same time that she had this chilling experience.

It should come as no surprise, then, that when Dean witnessed the attacks of September 11, she immediately associated them with Ressam. "It brought it all back—December 1999—just like a bomb. . . . Part of you knows that what you're watching isn't a movie," she adds, "but then part of you thinks, 'What am I watching?' I thought, 'These people are just evil. Look at the extent that they'll go to just to harm us.' It was almost numbing. When I saw that plane hit the tower, Ressam was the very first thing that I thought of."[22]

Dean credits her on-the-job experience as the key factor helping her to improve her interrogation and inspection skills. That experience, she said, taught her to always anticipate the situation—and never react to it. "I would look at the car behind the car I was actually talking to," she says, "just to kind of get an idea what was coming up."[23]

Experience also gave her a baseline by which to judge erratic behavior or conditions. Port Angeles was her third assignment as a customs inspector. Prior to that, she had worked in Hawaii and Seattle. Her husband, now deceased, worked as an inspector and in supervisory positions with the agency. At the time of her encounter with Ressam, she had worked in Port Angeles for a decade and had become very familiar with the kinds of travelers, tourists, and troublemakers who passed through her gate. "After ten years, everybody kind of starts to look alike—I don't care what country they come from or what the color of their skin is, and so you know what to expect in your port. So, when something stands out that isn't quite right for your port, you're going to take a little closer look at it."[24]

Dean assumes that in order to develop this instinctual sense of what's out of the ordinary, a border inspector must maintain a constant level of alertness. In other words, they already must have some basic hard-wiring for law enforcement. Dean believes that while some of the traits that make her a great inspector can be taught, a customs border patrol candidate must have some innate talent, some God-given ability. In short, a BS detector. "Absolutely. Not everybody is cut out to be in law enforcement, and certainly not everybody is cut out to be looking for the worst in people, or to be that curious about people." She added, "I think when I started that I had that curiosity. And I certainly always I had the desire [to be a Customs Inspector]. From the day that I started the job, I always felt that I was performing a valuable service to the country, whether that was simply getting people through my line fast." For Diana Dean, though, it was the day-in and day-out experience that she feels raised her level of ability. "You talk to so many people every day that you can get a feeling for what's true."[25]

Most fascinating about Diana Dean's experience with Ressam is her preparation—not a track record of facing extraordinary events, but just the opposite. Every day she would go through the standard questions and procedures over and over with thousands of people. And this routine sharpened, rather than dulled, her professional expertise. Former Navy Secretary and 9/11 Commissioner John

Lehman has spoken eloquently on several occasions about the need of our government bureaucracies to resist complacency. Dean should be a case study in these efforts. She wasn't distracted by the routine. Instead, she thrived on it, used it to her advantage, and became a better customs inspector for it. "You work in a place for a certain length of time," she says, "and you just know what the next car is going to have in it because it is pretty much just like the one in front of it, unless there's something wrong, and then by experience you know that this just isn't right."[26]

It would have been easy for Dean to simply rattle off the standard questions and then allow Ressam to go on his way. After all, it was late and Ressam's car was the very last one off the day's final ferry. And most of the ferry passengers had already been questioned once on the Canadian side of the border crossing. Asked whether this kind of innate suspicion was something that our government could train people to adopt, she responded, "I don't know if you could profile a person before you hire them [as a border inspector] to see if we have a different attitude than some or to see if we're more suspicious by nature, or more curious by nature." She added, "I think that training plays a very big part, [especially] role playing—you know, 'What if . . . ?' And thinking of all the things that could go wrong and all the different people that you're going to see."[27] And according to Dean, it's up to the government to "naturally select" those who have the innate abilities necessary to cautiously watch over the country's borders.

The story of the capture of Ahmed Ressam is surprising. How he arrived at that moment is also surprising—and galling. Consider that Ressam first entered the country via Mirabel Airport in Montreal on Feb. 24, 1994. Authorities easily spotted that his French passport was fraudulent. He claimed that the Algerian police had been after him and that his life was in danger. "Eleven days later he had an apartment in Montreal and was drawing welfare benefits," a *Boston Globe* account would later acknowledge.[28] Substantive inquiries should have been performed when this young Algerian male immigrated to Canada—and especially when he returned to Canada after spending eleven months training at an al-Qaeda camp in Afghanistan.[29]

Indeed, Canada by the late 1990s had become a popular haven—"because of its loose immigration procedures, lack of antiterrorism laws, and social welfare programs so generous that even someone arriving with falsified documents could count on drawing government checks within a few weeks,[30]" by one account—for dormant terrorists awaiting instruction from bin Laden. Morteda Zabouri, a Middle East specialist with the Universite de Montreal's research group in international security, described it this way: "Because we've never been bitten by the spider, Canada pays little attention as it spins webs in our house."[31]

After Ressam's plot was discovered and unraveled, the lack of attention Canadian antiterrorism authorities paid to those webs drew the ire of officials from the United States, Britain and France. That tension reached its boiling point after it was disclosed that Canadian officials had destroyed wiretap evidence against Ressam and his cohorts: "Apparently this is the Canadian way of doing things," remarked an incredulous U.S. District Judge John Coughenour, who presided over Ressam's trial in California. "I find [it] totally unacceptable."[32]

Of course, that was before September 11, 2001. And as the 9/11 Commission would report, America had mistakes of its own it needed to correct. The United States had to change its attitudes toward travel and border security in a world seemingly (and perhaps unknowingly) ridden with terrorists who wanted to do this country harm. And the government had to change the way it does business on the borders. Besides the massive restructuring brought about by the creation of the Department of Homeland Security, federal agencies have instituted more stringent passenger screening, up-to-the-minute watch lists for terrorists and criminals, and enhanced training for our border inspectors in the areas of interviewing and interrogation. These are just a few facets of the "new norm" in border protection, but they were not in place when Diana Dean met Ressam. Dean was—and is—a role model for keen instincts and sharp intuition. As Condoleezza Rice said, "I think it actually wasn't by chance . . . It was because a very alert customs agent named Diana Dean and her colleagues sniffed something about Ressam," Rice said. "They saw that something was wrong. They tried to apprehend him. He tried to run. They then apprehended him, found that there was bomb-making material and a map of Los Angeles."[33]

Indeed, the significance of Dean's instinct is even more remarkable because she had no prior warning that a terror plot was in the works. September 11 was still an event far in the future, and nobody was talking about Osama bin Laden or al-Qaeda. That wasn't the context in which she approached her job; she wasn't thinking in that direction. As she recalled, "Al-Qaeda was something I'd heard of, but certainly nothing that pertained to us. And when I saw Ressam as I glanced back at his car—there were only twenty cars on the ferry that night and his was the last car—I saw a lone male in a very nice car, and that just sort of pricks your instincts a little bit because it's unusual, or it was unusual for that time."[34] Yet she wasn't thinking about Middle Eastern terrorists when Ressam approached. In fact, she says, "He gave me his driver's license, and I could tell from the very first question I asked that he spoke French, and his license said that he was from Quebec, and I just assumed that he was French Canadian."[35] Later, when Ressam's trunk was opened, she first suspected drugs, not bomb-making materials, were enclosed. Indeed, the drug tests investigators performed that night were inconclusive. Only when they found what they thought to be timers in the car did they deduce that the powder was intended to be used in a bomb plot. "My heart dropped right into my toes when I realized what it was," Dean said. "I don't recall any specific threats," she continued. "I don't recall anybody saying watch for terrorists."[36]

That's why it's tough to argue with Elaine Kamarck, a lecturer at the Harvard University Kennedy School, who suggested that the best defense against terror is the cop on the beat. She asks, "How about some new jobs in the subways and on the borders?"[37] Dean's story perfectly illustrates why this would be a good idea. She spent ten years getting to know her "beat" in Port Angeles, Washington, and when Ahmed Ressam tried to slip by her, he failed. Subsequently, in April 2001, Ressam was convicted on nine counts, including conspiracy to commit an act of international terrorism, and sentenced to twenty-two years in prison.[38]

In fact, more than one terrorist was apprehended as a result of Diana Dean's work. During the early 2001 trial of his coconspirator Mokhtar Haouari, Ressam provided evidence that incriminated both Haouari and Hassan Zemiri. Haouari was convicted in January 2002 and is currently serving a twenty-four-year sentence for his role in the bomb plot.[39] A federal appeals panel upheld that conviction the following year.[40] As for Zemiri, Ressam testified that he had given him $3,500 and a camera so he'd look more like a tourist than a terrorist.[41] When Zemiri heard that Ressam was cooperating with U.S. authorities, he took his wife and fled from Montreal, Canada, to Afghanistan. As with Mohamed al-Kahtani, Zemiri was captured in the caves of Tora Bora in late 2001. He is now being detained as an enemy combatant at the U.S. military base in Guantanamo Bay, Cuba. Ressam's testimony was the basis for Zemiri's incarceration, the *Seattle Times* reported.[42]

In January 2007, however, Ressam attempted to recant his previous testimony, writing, "Mr. Hassan Zamiry [sic] is innocent and has no relation or connection to the operation I was about to carry out. He also did not know anything about it and he did not assist me in anything. It is true that I have borrowed some money and a camera from him, but this was only a personal loan between me and him. It has nothing to do with my case or support as the Prosecutor has alleged."[43] Ressam also complained to the judge that his initial account about Zemiri was given while he was "in shock and had a severe psychological disorder."[44] The case against Zemiri is still pending, though his capture in Tora Bora offers damning evidence which may lead to his conviction for terrorist sympathies and activities.

The parallels between Dean and Melendez-Perez are similar enough to suggest that those responsible for turning potential terrorists away at the border take innate abilities like "street smarts" more seriously and try to look for ways to instill and foster them in other border personnel. In summary, those parallels are listed below:

- Like Melendez-Perez, Dean had an immediate first-impression that something was just "not right" about the man in the expensive car pulling up to her inspection station in the tiny town of Port Angeles, Washington.
- Like Melendez-Perez, Dean had years of experience but was not looking for terrorists. When she and her colleagues eventually found garbage bags filled with bomb-making chemicals in Ressam's trunk, her first reaction was that he was a drug smuggler. Melendez-Perez, meanwhile, felt at first that Kahtani was a hit-man, not a terrorist.
- Like Melendez-Perez, Dean was tenacious. She pursued matters even when it meant putting her reputation on the line. Federal agents were resistant when they heard her story and initially unwilling to go "out in the middle of nowhere" to investigate Ressam.
- Like Melendez-Perez, Dean got "the creeps" from the man she was interviewing. At first, something just didn't fit, and she was struck by an even stronger feeling when she looked into Ressam's eyes.

DEVIL IN THE DETAILS

Charlie Hanger has always been "suspicious by nature."[45] So when the ten-year veteran Oklahoma highway patrol-man spotted a clunky old yellow 1977 Mercury Grand Marquis headed north on Interstate 35 near the town of Perry in Noble County, he immediately—and almost without having to think about it—took a closer look. Something was wrong about this old junker, and it didn't take long to spot it. The car was missing its license plate.

Officer Hanger had a lot on his mind that day—Wednesday, April 19, 1995. Like September 11, 2001, it was a day that dawned bright and serene. But then, at 9:02 a.m., the tranquility in the area surrounding the Alfred P. Murrah Federal Building in downtown Oklahoma City was eviscerated by an enormous explosion. According to subsequent FBI investigations, the bombers packed nearly five-thousand pounds of ammonium nitrate fertilizer and fuel oil into a rented Ryder truck and parked it outside the federal building, which contained not only a branch of the Bureau of Alcohol, Tobacco, and Firearms, but a United States Marine recruiting office and a children's day care facility.[46] Shockwaves from the explosion were felt as far as thirty miles away. The attack killed 168 people, 19 of whom were children.[47] About eight hundred more people were injured.[48]

The blast had occurred only seventy-eight minutes before Trooper Charles J. Hanger spotted the battered yellow Marquis about seventy miles away from the Murrah Building.[49] He had no idea that the man driving the car just carried out the attack in Oklahoma City. In fact, Hanger hadn't even considered that the explosion was an attack. "Not once did I think it was a terrorist attack—not in the heartland," he would say years later. Hanger drove south on I-35 after being dispatched to Oklahoma City, only to turn around after receiving a second order to stay put. Driving back north, he stopped to help two women who'd gotten a flat tire. After calling a wrecker, he proceeded north and was about to exit the highway when he spotted the 1977 Mercury. Though preoccupied with the events that had occurred downtown, Trooper Hanger decided to take a closer look at the car he had just passed.[50]

According to Melinda Henneberger of the *New York Times*, who interviewed Hanger's Perry, Oklahoma, friends,[51] this was a trooper who was "unyielding" and "firm" when attending to his highway patrol duties. "'He'd arrest his own mother for a traffic violation,' Hanger's friend Bill Gengler said." Another friend recalled that Hanger had once pulled him over for driving fifty-seven miles per hour in a fifty-five-mph zone. "He's the epitome of what you expect a law enforcement officer to be because he always goes strictly by the book," another Perry native said. Almost everyone who knew Charlie Hanger, it seemed, said "he is one of those guys who always seems to be on the job." "He even comes to church in his uniform," a local Perry pastor noted at the time. In other words, Hanger is straight out of *No Country for Old Men*.

According to the sworn testimony he later gave in Timothy McVeigh's trial, Trooper Hanger pulled the 1977 Grand Marquis over without incident after noting that it was missing its license plate. The driver didn't have the tags (or a bill of sale for the vehicle for that matter), he told Hanger, because he had purchased the vehicle just recently. When asked to produce his driver's license, the man complied. It read: Timothy James McVeigh.[52]

And though Trooper Hanger will never forget reading that name for the first time, it is not the only thing he noticed at the time. As McVeigh handed him his driver's license, Hanger noticed a "bulge" under the man's jacket on the left side of his body. He testified in court: "I told him to take both hands and slowly pull back his jacket." In a cooperative tone of voice, McVeigh replied, "I have a gun."[53]

Trooper Hanger then "reached for the bulge on the jacket and grabbed it. I pulled my weapon and stuck it to the back of his head," he recounted in court. He then guided McVeigh toward the back of his car, where the trooper removed the pistol and a pouch that contained an extra clip. Remaining cooperative, McVeigh informed him that he was also carrying a knife, and Hanger removed this as well before handcuffing him. When asked why he was carrying a weapon, McVeigh said, according to Hanger, that he had the right to do so to protect himself. Up to this point, Trooper Hanger made no connection between the bombing and the man he had apprehended.[54]

Indeed, Hanger told Mark Gibson, assistant district attorney for Noble County, that McVeigh was polite throughout their interaction, addressing the trooper as "Sir" and assuring him he meant no harm. Less than an hour after that initial confrontation, Hanger had also concluded that McVeigh's story wasn't right—though he still didn't know what McVeigh's real crime had been. "But the way Charlie's mind works—he's suspicious by nature—when he stopped [McVeigh], he asked him, 'Where are you from?' and when he said Michigan and he was driving across the country, that made him suspicious right away," Gibson explained, "because he said nobody drives across country with a suit jacket on. Then later he saw he didn't have any luggage."[55]

Trooper Hanger's gut told him that something was particularly wrong about McVeigh's explanation for carrying a weapon because "he was always on the road." As Gibson of the district attorney's office explained, "When he grabbed his gun and there was no reaction, no shock, that didn't seem right, either. Neither did his story. Charlie said, 'If you were in the military, when were you a security guard?' and he said when he was on vacation. So things didn't really jibe."[56]

Hanger was able to book him on five misdemeanor charges, including unlawfully carrying a concealed firearm and transporting a loaded firearm in a motor vehicle. Hanger's thoroughness would prove pivotal in cracking the bombing case. His arrest effectively detained McVeigh until federal authorities could track down the information they had found about the rental truck used in the bombing.

There was also a bit of luck involved: Judge Danny Allen's crowded calendar—he couldn't hear McVeigh's case because he was dealing with a divorce case at the time— postponed McVeigh's release on bail.[57] So, McVeigh was still in jail, though just "thirty minutes from being released . . . when the FBI called to ask if local authorities had the suspect to match the Social Security number on the phony driver's license that Mr. McVeigh was using when Mr. Hanger stopped him."[58]

A hardened Timothy McVeigh would later blame the government's measures at Waco and at Ruby Ridge for his actions.[59] McVeigh had visited Waco at the time of the standoff between Branch Davidians and federal agents, and apparently even publicly expressed his outrage to a news reporter.[60] It's clear that both McVeigh and his accomplice, Terry Nichols, harbored sympathies for the antigovernment militia movement.

Their twisted views plainly baffled Hanger. "I dream about what he did. It's just beyond me how anyone could knowingly take children's lives. That's just beyond me," he said. Hanger had, for a while, sent his family out of town in fear of retribution from McVeigh's coconspirators or sympathizers. As it turned out, though, he could thankfully move on with his life—and perhaps became even more appreciative of life because of the danger he and his family faced. "I've changed. Since then, the people I love in my life, I don't hesitate to tell them that. I'm just thankful for everything," he said.[61]

Before that fateful day in April 1995, Trooper Hanger had already been highly decorated for the professionalism with which he carried out his job. He is a former recipient of both the Oklahoma Highway Patrol Outstanding DUI Enforcement Award and the Outstanding Drug Interdiction Efforts Award. And as a result of the actions he took to arrest Timothy McVeigh, the Oklahoma Highway Users Federation named him Trooper of the Year for 1995. He also received a commendation from New York City Mayor Rudy Giuliani. First Lieutenant Jim McBride, Trooper Hanger's immediate supervisor, stated: "Trooper Hanger's a real team player. He is crucial to the success of the criminal interdiction unit in Oklahoma. He always pays close attention to details. He constantly looks out for and takes care of his troopers." Not surprisingly, Hanger has been promoted twice since 1995, most recently to the rank of Second Lieutenant.[62] "What I did was not heroic," Hanger said. "I was thankful the good Lord looked after me and kept me safe. I just was doing my job the way thousands of other troopers around the country do their jobs every day. I will say that on that day the good Lord put me in the right place at the right time and He took care of me while I was there."[63]

The motto of this God-fearing lawman from the plains is, rather appropriately, "Take care of the small things, the big things will come to you."[64] Fittingly, a tag snag tripped up the perpetrator of the deadliest act of domestic terrorism ever committed in the United States. Similarly, Mohamed al-Kahtani's dirty look led Jose Melendez-Perez to probe deeper into the circumstances of the young Saudi's travel to the United States. And Diana Dean's assessment of a strange circumstance led to the incarceration of the man driving a luxury car through tiny, out-of-the-way Port Angeles, Washington, on his "visit" to Seattle.

A WEIRD DUCK

*Hello, Mrs. Matt, I am Mrs. Zacarias. Basically I need
to know if you can help to achieve my "goal" my dream.
I would like to fly in a "professional" like manners one of
the big airliners. The level I would like to achieve is to be
able to takeoff and land, to handle communication with
ATC [air-traffic control]. . . . In a sense, to be able to pilot
one of these Big Bird, even if I am not a real professional
pilot.*[65]

This strange, poorly written e-mail was received by Matthew Tierney at the Pan Am International Flight Academy in Eagan, Minnesota, in May 2001. It came from somebody using a Hotmail account named "zulu mantangotango." And, no, it wasn't spam. The e-mail's author was thirty-three-year-old Zacarias Moussaoui, a French national of Moroccan descent.

The real story is how the instinct of several Americans foiled his "dream."

The Pan Am school in Minnesota was not Moussaoui's first attempt at flight training. From February 26 to May 29, 2000, Moussaoui attended flight-training courses at Airman Flight School in Norman, Oklahoma, with the goal of earning Cessna certification. Despite more than fifty hours of flying lessons, he did not pass and left without a pilot's license.[66] Airman was also visited by Mohamed Atta and Marwan al-Shehhi, the hijacker pilots who flew their planes into the north and south towers of the World Trade Center, respectively. For whatever reason, Atta and al-Shehhi decided instead to pursue their pilot training at Huffman Aviation in Venice, Florida.[67] Undaunted by his failure at the Cessna school, Moussaoui pleaded with the staff in Minnesota, "I know it could be better but I am sure that you can do something. After all we are in AMERICA, and everything is possible."[68] As terrorism expert Daniel Pipes has said, "The cynicism and falsehood of the Islamists knows no bounds."[69] Yet Moussaoui's arrogant cynicism—like that of Mohamed al-Kahtani—was his undoing.

Moussaoui's journey into radical Islam most likely began in London's Finsbury Park mosque under the tutelage of extremist Abu Hamza. Though they never charged him with any crime, French authorities did begin monitoring Moussaoui in the 1990s after he traveled to Pakistan and Afghanistan several times and began "sounding fanatic."[70] He traveled to Khalden to attend the terrorist training camp there, and in 2000 stayed in a condo that had been the site of an al-Qaeda meeting (attended by two of the September 11) hijackers just months before.[71] Months later, he arrived in the United States, where "everything is possible," and his perverse American dream made him eager to fly. The Pan Am academy accepted him as they had so many other Middle Eastern applicants, and in early August of 2001, Moussaoui began instruction in Eagan, which is not far from Minneapolis.

But it wasn't long before he began to raise suspicions among the staff—beginning with the fact that he paid $8,300—most of it in hundred-dollar bills—for lessons in flying a 747 jumbo jet.[72] FBI agents later surmised that the cash probably came from the $14,000 in wire transfers Moussaoui received from Ramzi bin al-Shibh originating from Dusseldorf and Hamburg, Germany.[73]

Hiding the fact that he was a Muslim, Moussaoui told the flight school staff that he wanted to take a simulated flight from New York's John F. Kennedy Airport to London's Heathrow Airport. "In a sense, to be able to pilot one of these

Big Bird, even if I am not a real professional pilot," he wrote in his e-mail. Tim Nelson, head of the engineering courses for 727s and 747s, wasn't buying it—not after hearing about the cash the new student had produced to pay his fees and the fact that he didn't have a pilot's license. Hugh Sims, a veteran pilot with a Texas drawl, was also giving the hairy eyeball to the newcomer.

Like Jose Melendez-Perez, Nelson and Sims have extensive military backgrounds. A veteran of more than twenty years in the Air Force, Nelson served as a B-52 gunner in the Persian Gulf War—often flying in aircrafts carrying nuclear weapons. By his retirement he'd attained the rank of master sergeant. Sims flew 150 missions during the Vietnam War and himself spent twenty-four years in the Air Force.[74]

Given their backgrounds, it's not surprising that they asked some probing questions. "He's going to pay us to get some 747-400 orientation and he's not any more than a private pilot?" Sims asked. "Why would a guy do that? Why would you spend that much money, other than you just want to do this as a lark?"[75] Nelson, the Air Force vet, was separately making his own inquiries. "Oh, you mean he's buying a joy ride, one sim period?" he asked the pilot training manager. When he was told that no, in fact, Moussaoui had paid for a couple of days worth of classroom training as well as several sessions in the 747 flight simulator, Nelson was baffled. Why would a guy with no pilot's license come to America and pay a bunch of cash to fly a jumbo jet? Inquiring about Moussaoui's background, Nelson was told that the foreigner was "an international businessman."[76] Which reminded the Air Force veteran of a movie entitled "Security First" that a Japan-based airline had previously sent to the school. The film detailed an incident that occurred less than two years before in which a man hijacked one of the airline's planes, killed the captain, and circled over Tokyo before the cocaptain wrestled the controls away. "Do we have one of these guys or what?" Nelson said to himself. He personally went and pulled Moussaoui's file to check his flying experience. It was practically empty.[77]

Moussaoui showed up at the Minnesota flight school on August 13, 2001, wearing a red T-shirt, baseball cap, jeans, and tennis shoes. He hadn't forgotten to closely trim his beard either. But for all his efforts, he immediately impressed his instructor, a retired Northwest captain named Clancy Prevost, as "just a weird duck."[78] Sims and Nelson also noted Moussaoui's appearance, observing that it wasn't consistent with that of an "international businessman" spending loads of dough. "OK, ratty jeans, ratty shirt, ratty hat," Nelson thought. "If he's dropping that kind of money to play, I'm expecting to see Rolexes and Guccis." Fueling these suspicions was the report of Jerry Liddell, the school's accountant, who told McHale, the flight-training supervisor, that even though Moussaoui had paid for the bulk of his fees with nearly seven thousand dollars–worth of cash, he was nevertheless a few hundred short—and had no credit card to handle the difference. What kind of international businessman travels without a credit card? McHale called company headquarters with his concerns, but they insisted that paying customers be left alone. Besides, it was argued, the desire of foreigners to come to U.S. flight schools and pay a lot of cash to take "joy rides" was commonplace. Moussaoui's behavior, in short, appeared to be business as usual.[79]

Prevost, Moussaoui's instructor, found his new pupil amiable, if a bit secretive about his past. During casual chitchat, he asked Moussaoui if he was a Muslim. "Prevost described Moussaoui's reaction as being one of surprise and caution," an FBI affidavit read. "When he recovered, Moussaoui informed him that he was not a Muslim." Coming to his own conclusions, Hugh Sims didn't believe Moussaoui had thousands of dollars to spend on flight lessons—international businessman or not. "This is a perfect guy to want to hijack an airplane," he thought at the time.[80] By the second day of Moussaoui's training, the Pan Am training staff had begun to compare notes, and the bottom line was the same. Recalling that his new understudy had asked whether it was possible for a pilot to shut off oxygen to the passengers, Prevost told the training supervisor, "There's really something wrong with this guy."[81] Nelson, meanwhile, was telling supervisor McHale the same thing. During lunch he had observed Moussaoui speaking in Arabic with two Syrian Airlines pilots who happened to pass by. "How's his Arabic?" Nelson asked the Syrians, out of earshot of Moussaoui. "Oh, he's fluent," they said. "He's a native speaker." Nelson sighed to himself. "Oh great. One more strike."[82]

By the end of Moussaoui's second day at the Minnesota flight school, Nelson and Sims had separately come to the conclusion that federal authorities needed to be notified. But they faced supervisors and company headquarters personnel who didn't want any trouble. "I knew Hugh was pretty much on board," Nelson said. "The other guys, they agreed. But everybody was kind of looking down at their feet, shuffling back and forth."[83] The following day, Nelson and Sims took action. In its exclusive interview with the two men, the *Star Tribune* told it this way:

> *At 8:30 a.m. while sitting in his cubicle at Pan Am, Nelson dialed the FBI's Minneapolis office. He was quickly passed to Dave Rapp, an agent in the counterterrorism unit.*

*I said, 'Here's my position,' Nelson recalled. 'I'm call-
ing on a customer. I'm sticking my neck out. I'm going to
either be a hero or a goat. If I'm wrong, it's probably going
to cost me my job.'*

*He said he had concluded that, given his suspicions,
he would 'rather call and be wrong than not call and be
right.'*

*He shared his hunches about Moussaoui with Rapp
and told him:*

*'I don't know if you remember, but there was an El-Al
Airlines 747 freighter that took off out of Amsterdam that
had a mechanical problem and crashed into an apartment
complex. Here's the problem: You've got an aircraft that
weighs upwards of 900,000 pounds fully loaded and car-
ries between 50,000 and 57,000 gallons of jet fuel. If you
fly it at 350 knots [about 400 miles per hour] into a heavily
populated area, you're going to kill a boatload of people.'*

*Describing his military background, he gave Rapp his
cell phone number. 'I want to assure you that I'm not a
kook,' Nelson said he told Rapp.*

*About an hour later, while having breakfast with his
wife, Nancy, in their St. Paul apartment, Sims said: 'I just
can't stand this.'*

*Operating under the military motto, 'Don't ask
a question if you can't stand a 'no' answer,' he decided
against seeking the school's permission and dialed the
FBI.*

*Before noon, FBI agents were at McHale's office, ask-
ing about Moussaoui.*[84]

Moussaoui was arrested on August 16, 2001, for immigration violations. Later, after the September 11 attacks, he was
indicted on six counts of conspiracy to, among other things,

"murder thousands of innocent people in New York, Virginia, and Pennsylvania."[85] Moussaoui eventually pleaded guilty to all six charges of conspiracy, four of which carried the possibility of the death penalty. He stated his intention to take part in a follow-up attack on the United States after September 11. "I came to the United States of America to be part, O.K., of a conspiracy to use airplane as a weapon of mass destruction, a statement of fact to strike the White House, but this conspiracy was a different conspiracy than 9/11," he said.[86]

It's easy to look back on Moussaoui's behavior at the Minnesota flight school with the hindsight of our post-September 11 experience. But the country should not lose sight of the bravery of the flight school staff members who were willing to drop the dime on this wannabe jihadist—to risk their jobs and reputations on the fact that a foreigner was up to no good. On May 17, 2005, the U.S. Senate rightly honored Tim Nelson and Hugh Sims. "Our country owes these men a debt of gratitude for their attentiveness and courage, which may have preempted another attack and saved thousands of lives," said Senator Mark Dayton (D-Minnesota), who coauthored the resolution with Senator Norm Coleman (R-Minnesota). Coleman added: "As we continue to grieve those whom we lost in the aftermath of September 11, we realize the enormous impact and importance of [Nelson's and Sims'] actions."[87] Sims maintained, "My part in it was relatively small . . . It was just a phone call."[88] Nelson said he was "flattered and honored" by the resolution. "We were just trying to do the things that people should do day in and day out."[89]

Their humility should not lead the nation to lose sight of the fact that the government must continue to look for ways to reward the proper and reasonable vigilance of its citizens. After all, the reality is that terrorists will try to attack the United States again as they did on September 11. Captured al-Qaeda members later told U.S. interrogators that Moussaoui was never intended to be a part of the World Trade Center and Pentagon attacks, but was training for a later attack on the White House. It's clear that further acts of terrorism are still being plotted. But is the country working to prevent them? As it turns out, just a few days after Moussaoui's arrest, Tim Nelson was giving instruction to three FAA examiners. When he told them about Moussaoui, they were skeptical. "What did [Moussaoui] do that's illegal?" the examiners asked, according to Nelson. He recalled one of the inspectors chiming in cynically: "We're the tombstone agency. We don't do anything until there's a tombstone."[90]

If the staff of the Minnesota flight school pondered whether they had a madman on their hands, there was no question that spectators and jury members at Zacarias Moussaoui's trial were quite sure of it. After all, they even had the words of the captured 9/11 mastermind, Khalid Sheikh Mohammed, to back it up. In the transcript of an interrogation read aloud in court, KSM declared Moussaoui too "problematic" and unreliable to participate in the September 11 offensive.[91] Instead, KSM was apparently grooming Moussaoui "for a second wave of attacks." In late March 2006, Moussaoui—despite repeated protests of his own court-appointed lawyers—took the stand and testified that Richard Reid, who would later be arrested after trying to blow up an airplane using explosives he'd hidden in his shoes, had been contracted to hijack a fifth plane on September 11:

"Before your arrest, were you scheduled to pilot a plane as part of the 9/11 operation?" defense attorney Gerald

Zerkin asked his client. "Yes. I was supposed to pilot a plane to hit the White House," Moussaoui replied. . . .

Prosecutor Robert Spencer asked, "You knew on Aug. 16 that other Al Qaeda members were in the United States?" "That's correct," Moussaoui replied. Spencer: "You knew there was a pending plot?" "That's correct." Spencer: "You lied because you wanted to conceal that you were a member of al-Qaeda?" "That's correct." "You lied so the plan could go forward?" "That's correct."[92]

The testimony was a virtual death wish. "If jurors believe that Moussaoui was scheduled for the September 11 mission, it would be easier for them to conclude that he did bear responsibility for the deaths that day," Richard Serrano explained in the *Los Angeles Times*. "Arrested weeks before the attacks, he presumably would have known enough about the plot to head it off by cooperating with the FBI. Prosecutors argue that would make him eligible for the death penalty."[93] The threat of capital punishment hardly seemed to discourage Moussaoui, who told the court he rejoiced to hear the news of the World Trade Center attacks while sitting in a Minnesota jail cell. "I'm not concerned with the death penalty," he said. "I don't believe you have or the government or the jury will have anything to say about my death . . . I believe in destiny." And he openly bragged, "You don't have to be trained to cut the throat of somebody . . . It is not difficult." In fact, Moussaoui admitted that he purchased several small knives with the intention of taking down "a passenger or flight attendant or anyone else who got in his way."[94]

The implication of shoe bomber Richard Reid as a fellow hijacker of his supposed fifth plane is not quite as far-fetched as it might seem, since both men attended the extremist Finsbury Park Mosque in London.[95] Still, no further evidence exists to suggest they knew one another, or that Reid was in the United States in August. But Moussaoui's alleged ties to Reid were only one of many tangled threads that made the case bizarre, fascinating, and complex. The court would have to weigh the defendant's March 2006 admission of 9/11 coconspiracy against his own previous contradictory statements. In a court motion unsealed in July of 2002, Moussaoui wrote, "I am a terrorist in your eyes (as terrorism is like beauty, it is in the eye of the beholder). But it does not mean that I took part in Sept. 11. And the FBI know it as they were monitoring all my movement and communication for quite a long time in the U.S. and abroad."[96] Then a month later he stated, "I have no participation in Sept. 11, but . . . I have certain knowledge about Sept. 11, and I know exactly who done it." Nearly three years later, in March 2005, Moussaoui said, "I don't know the exact number of planes, but I was not the fifth [pilot] hijacker." He continued: "I had knowledge that the Twin Towers would be hit. I didn't know the details of this."[97] By late March 2006, however, he was denying that he was part of a second-wave attack and boasted that he was to take part in 9/11: "I was supposed to pilot a plane to hit the White House."[98]

Even if his exact role or level of knowledge is never ascertained, the drama of an admitted al-Qaeda member boasting of his own involvement in America's worst day is damning enough. "The familiar Moussaoui was gone," wrote the *Washington Post* regarding his court testimony. "In his place was a hardened terrorist operative who spoke calmly and methodically, looking straight at his questioners as he voiced his hatred for the nation that had put him on trial for his life. 'I consider every American to be my enemy,' Moussaoui, 37, said as jurors leaned forward in their seats. 'For me, every

American is going to want my death because I want their death.'" When asked by prosecutor Robert Spencer if he still believed (as he had written earlier) that "the 19 hijackers should be 'blessed' by Allah," Moussaoui unhesitatingly replied "One hundred percent." He also testified that he changed his mind about participating in the 9/11 attacks (at first he spurned al-Qaeda leaders' requests in 1999 for his participation) after dreaming about flying a plane into the White House. After Moussaoui told bin Laden about the dream, the al-Qaeda leader sent him to take flight training in the U.S. "The prosecution's best hope was to make him appear scary rather than crazy. It sounds like he was scary," said Eric Muller, a former federal prosecutor who teaches at the University of North Carolina.[99]

Moussaoui's defense team countered with the written testimony of other captured al-Qaeda plotters who dismissed Moussaoui's supposed role in the 9/11 plot. Because Moussaoui had, according to this testimony, "breached security measures and al-Qaida protocol" he was considered a "loose cannon" by bin Laden's terrorist organization. Walid bin Attash specified that Moussaoui indiscreetly called him on several occasions, "despite instructions to call only in an emergency," so he had his cell phone turned off. Bin Attash, considered the driving force behind the attack on the USS *Cole* and the al-Qaeda operative who influenced the selection of many of the September 11 hijackers, said Moussaoui was not training for a part in the 9/11 attacks.[100] Another captured terrorist, identified as Sayf al-Adl, a senior member of al-Qaeda's military committee, told U.S. interrogators that Moussaoui was "a confirmed jihadist but was absolutely not going to take part in the Sept. 11, 2001, mission."[101] Mustafa al-Hawsawi, the al-Qaeda financier, said that while he'd seen

Moussaoui at the terrorist safe house in Kandahar, they'd never met or collaborated. (Al-Hawsawi did, in fact, implicate Mohamed al-Kahtani as one of the names on his payroll of would-be hijackers.).[102]

The testimonies of the personal horrors of September 11 presented during Moussaoui's trial were riveting and emotional. A former firefighter saw a close friend die after a falling body landed on him. A police officer's wife died evacuating people from a burning building. Former New York City Mayor Rudy Giuliani told the courtroom: "It was the worst experience of my life . . . It meant the loss of friends I can't possibly replace. . . . Every day I think about it; every day, a part of it comes back to me. It can be the people jumping, the body parts, seeing a little boy or girl at a funeral." One of Moussaoui's lawyers welled up during the session. Sitting amongst the jurors were several boxes of tissues, reporters from the *Washington Post* noted.[103] Yet emotions could not be contained, and in fact reached a crescendo during the testimony of a woman who had stayed in a hotel near the twin towers and captured the horrors of that day on videotape. "Tamar Rosbrook tried her best to remain stoic," the *Washington Post* report continued, "as the television monitors showed person after person jumping from the World Trade Center and aiming for an awning in the plaza below. She tried to narrate the video she shot September 11, 2001, so the jury could understand what happened that day. But as prosecutors pointed out the body parts and the people on fire, she—and many of those in the courtroom—lost it. The sobs were uncontrollable and contagious."[104]

There was one man in the room, however, who was laughing at what he saw: the defendant, Zacarias Moussaoui.

"If he wasn't looking bored or glancing at the clock, he was smiling—especially when prosecutors played more than ten video clips that showed the hijacked planes hitting the towers and the buildings burning and crashing to the ground. And when his attorney offered condolences to Giuliani for 'the many losses you have suffered,' Moussaoui furiously shook his head," Jerry Markon and Timothy Dwyer wrote in the *Washington Post*.[105] Moussaoui grinned even as prosecutors presented "the final words of a woman who worked on the 83rd floor of the trade center and who called 911 while huddled on the floor. 'The floor is completely engulfed . . . we're on the floor, and we can't breathe and it's very, very hot. All I see is smoke. I'm going to die, aren't I? I'm going to die.' "[106] Defense attorney Gerald Zerkin did his best to try to dissuade the jury from reacting emotionally to the many witness testimonies—wanting them to focus instead on Moussaoui's troubled childhood and mental instability. He countered the prosecution's case by insisting that his client suffered from paranoid schizophrenia. "The government's evidence will present an extraordinary challenge for you," Zerkin said in his opening statement. "Nevertheless, you must open yourselves to the possibility of a sentence other than death."[107]

There was one more first-person account that the government had yet to present in its case against Moussaoui, which impacted the courtroom even more profoundly than previous heartrending accounts: the testimony of the passengers and crew of United Airlines Flight 93 themselves. The jury would hear not merely the reading of the transcript of the final minutes of that doomed flight, but the actual audio recordings obtained from the plane's flight data recorders and previously played only for federal investigators and select relatives.

On May 3, 2006—after hearing the heartbreaking first-hand accounts and unprecedented film and audio recordings of the deadliest terrorist attack on the United States and deliberating for over more than forty-one hours—the jury announced its stunning verdict: life in a maximum security prison for the man whose cooperation with authorities could have prevented 9/11. "My brother had his throat slit with the very kind of knives that Moussaoui secreted on his person," said Debra Burlingame, whose brother was the pilot of the plane hijacked and slammed into the Pentagon. She concluded, "It is ridiculous to say that because he was sitting in jail that he was somehow not responsible . . . This guy was absolutely a hard-core terrorist." Pointing out the fact that the Moussaoui verdict could inspire other Muslim extremists to take hostages and demand his release, Burlingame also stated, "I think it is very dangerous to show compassion to the cruel because they will bring cruelty to the compassionate." [108]

The arrest of Zacarias Moussaoui may not have required the kind of intuitive detective work we've seen in the cases of Jose Melendez-Perez and Diana Dean. There are, however, important similarities. Tim Nelson, Hugh Sims, and their colleagues at the Pan Am flight school in Minnesota were clearly attentive by nature and had years of military training and experience. Just as important was their willingness to speak up once they felt strong yet unpopular misgivings about Moussaoui and the large amounts of cash he was throwing around. The strange foreigner was not immediately threatening in the manner of Mohamed al-Kahtani or Ahmed Ressam, and yet they gradually became certain over a period of days that something was out of place—just wasn't right—about this "weird duck."

SECOND THOUGHTS

In *Blink: The Power of Thinking Without Thinking*, Malcolm Gladwell argues "that the power of first impressions suggests that human beings have a particular kind of prerational ability for making searching judgments about others." He terms this instantaneous capacity "thin slicing," which as one critic of the book explained, is a "positive new spin on the old practice of judging a book by its cover."[109] According to Gladwell, a "thin slice" is more than intuition or emotional gut reaction. It is thinking, he said. "It's just thinking that moves a little faster and operates a little more mysteriously than the kind of deliberate, conscious decision-making that we usually associate with 'thinking.'" He explained, "What we are picking up in that first instant would seem to be something quite basic about a person's character, because what we conclude after two seconds is pretty much the same as what we conclude after twenty minutes" or, indeed, months later. Gladwell then added, "In a way, that's comforting, because it suggests that we can meet a perfect stranger and immediately pick up on something important about him. It means that I shouldn't be concerned that I can't explain why I like [a given person], because, if such judgments are made without thinking, then surely they defy explanation."[110]

But Gladwell is also uncomfortable with his discoveries, and he worries that these first impressions might be too powerful—"that those initial impressions matter too much—that they color all the other impressions that we gather over time."[111] This anxiety over stereotypes and deep-seated biases has caused Gladwell's critics, like celebrated Judge Richard A. Posner from the University of Chicago Law School, to charge that his book is blinkered when it comes to racial realities: "It would not occur to Gladwell, a good liberal, that an auto salesman's discriminating on the basis of race or sex might be a rational form of the 'rapid cognition' that he admires . . . [I]t may be sensible to ascribe the group's average characteristics to each member of the group, even though one knows that many members deviate from the average. An individual's characteristics may be difficult to determine in a brief encounter, and a salesman cannot afford to waste his time in a protracted one, and so he may quote a high price to every black shopper even though he knows that some blacks are just as shrewd and experienced car shoppers as the average white, or more so. Economists use the term 'statistical discrimination' to describe this behavior."[112]

Whether Gladwell's findings may be questioned because of widespread racial and other stereotyping, *Blink* repeatedly demonstrates that even when our first impressions are correct, thinking can get in the way of rapid cognition. Our "thin slice," or intuitive glimpse into the behavior and character of another person, can be overwhelmed by events or suppressed by a guilty conscience. Instinct can vanish just as rapidly as it appeared—in the blink of an eye.

Just ask Michael Tuohey. Everybody can recall an unusually awful day at work that stands out beyond all others. For Michael Tuohey, that day was undoubtedly September 11, 2001—the day Tuohey said he "stared the devil in the eyes and didn't recognize him."[113]

The day began as most others did in his thirty-four-year career working as an airline ticket agent. Being an Army vet, Tuohey thrived on routine. Every morning at 3:30 a.m. he would wake up and—careful not to disturb his wife's sleep—quietly make his way to the kitchen. The coffee machine Tuohey had preset the night before was kindly offering him the day's first cup hot coffee. He took it, gratefully, and reached for the TV remote control to check the weather forecast and the CNN headlines. Then he would feed his cat, jump in the car, and head to work.

Tuohey worked for US Airways, a job that he had first held when the company was still Allegheny Airlines. His "office" at Portland International Jetport was about fifteen minutes from home. This normally gave him plenty of time to arrive, settle in, and continue to let the morning's coffee take effect before the big push of morning travelers flying from this small Maine airport to the Northeast's major cities would begin. Typically the crowds would pick up between 6:00 and 7:30 a.m., but something happened at 5:43 a.m. on that Tuesday morning that Michael Tuohey couldn't seem to forget.

With only seventeen minutes to spare before their flight to Boston, two young men wearing sport coats and ties approached his ticket counter. Looking back, Tuohey speculates that their late arrival was deliberate since they spent the night before at the Comfort Inn only a few minutes down the road. This would have allowed them to exploit an airline mentality that was then "more concerned about on-time departure than effective screening," Tuohey said.[114]

The pair immediately struck Tuohey as peculiar. Each man was in possession of a first-class, one-way ticket to Los Angeles via Boston—a $2,500 investment. "You don't see many of those," Tuohey acknowledged. The other reason the men stood out is less quantifiable and more difficult to convey. "It was just the look on the one man's face, his eyes," Tuohey told me. "By now, everyone in America has seen a picture of this man, but there is more life in that photograph we've all seen than he had in the flesh and blood. He looked like a walking corpse. He looked so angry. And he wouldn't look directly at me."[115]

The man was Mohamed Atta. And we're all familiar with the picture Tuohey refers to: that death mask of a face belonging to the leader of those nineteen fanatics. Tuohey described Atta's sidekick, Abdul Aziz al Omari, as a young man with "a goofy smile." "I can't believe he knew he was going to die that day," he added, clearly astonished.[116]

Tuohey remembers certain aspects of what was going through his mind during that eerie encounter. "I looked up, and asked them the standard questions. The one guy was looking at me. It sent a chill through me. Something in my stomach churned. And subconsciously, I said to myself, 'If they don't look like Arab terrorists, nothing does.'"[117]

Tuohey's next thought is significant: "Then I gave myself a mental slap. In over thirty-four years, I had checked in thousands of Arab travelers and I never thought this before. I said to myself, 'That's not nice to think. They are just two Arab businessmen.'"[118] Having checked himself for his presumptive thoughts, he handed them their boarding passes.

Once out of sight, the jackets and ties were gone. As the file footage that the cable news channels would show endlessly in the days after the attacks, Atta and Omari passed through the metal detectors wearing open neck dress shirts. At 6:45 a.m., the two men rendezvoused with the rest of their terrorist team: Satam al Suqami, Wail al Shehri and Waleed al Shehri. The five then checked in and boarded American Airlines Flight 11 bound for LA. The flight was scheduled to depart at 7:45 a.m. It actually departed at 7:59 a.m. At 8:46 a.m., it hit the North Tower.

Michael Tuohey remembers hearing the news of the "crash" back in Portland, Maine. "One of the agents from another airline said, 'Did you hear what happened in New York? I said, 'Oh my God!' and I was sorry I had judged [the two men]. I thought it was an accident."[119]

Then United Airlines Flight 175 hit the South Tower, at 9:03 a.m., and Michael Tuohey knew his first instinct had been correct. "As soon as someone told me news of the second flight, I had a knot in my stomach," he recalled.[120]

CHAPTER FIVE

LET'S ROLL

There were forty-four people aboard United Airlines Flight 93 on the morning of September 11, 2001, which means only about 20 percent of its 182 seats were filled.[1] That wasn't a coincidence. In fact, the hijackers purposely chose flights with relatively low numbers of passengers all the way to the west coast. Why? Because in theory, they would offer the least amount of resistance to the terrorists' plans to harness thousands of gallons of explosive jet fuel to commit as many murders and cause as much destruction as possible. (The 757 of American Airlines Flight 77, which struck the Pentagon, was only carrying 58 passengers.)[2] According to the 9/11 Commission Report, Flight 93 pulled away from its gate at Newark International Airport on time, but was held up by the airport's typical rush of morning traffic. It finally took off at 8:42 a.m.—four minutes before American Airlines Flight 11 hit the North Tower of the World Trade Center and approximately twenty-five minutes behind schedule.[3]

Though Captain Jason Dahl and First Officer LeRoy Homer had been flying since they were teenagers, they had never flown together before September 11. Dahl was a United Airlines pilot and trainer. Homer was an Air Force veteran of Desert Storm. They were accompanied by purser Deborah Jacobs Welsh; Lorraine Bay, who'd served as a flight attendant for thirty-seven years; Wanda Anita Green, set to retire after almost thirty years working in the airline industry; and CeeCee Lyles, a former police officer who'd been a flight attendant for just nine months. Also part of the crew was Sandra Bradshaw, who was working one of the two trips she typically flew per month—a limit she adhered to so she could stay home with her two small children.[4]

The passengers represented a cross section of Americans (though not all were U.S. residents) whose ages ranged from twenty to seventy-nine. The youngest passenger, Deora Frances Bodley, had been visiting friends on the east coast and was then beginning her junior year in college. Hilda Marcin, the eldest, was heading to California to live with her daughter. Todd Beamer, an account manager with Oracle who had just returned from a five-day vacation to Italy with his wife, was embarking on a one-day business trip. Patrick "Joe" Driscoll and William Cashman were friends bound for Yosemite National Park for their annual hiking trip. Joseph DeLuca and his girlfriend Linda Gronlund planned to celebrate her birthday in California's wine country. Jeremy Glick was leaving behind a three-month-old daughter to attend a business meeting. Nicole Miller had been in New York and New Jersey sightseeing with her friends. She was supposed to head home to California on September 10 to start college, but thunderstorms forced that flight's cancellation, so she was rescheduled for Flight 93. John Talignani was on his way to his stepson's memorial service. He had been killed just days earlier in a car accident while on his honeymoon in California. Mark Bingham was the last passenger to board to the plane. He was en route home to San Francisco, where he was scheduled to be an usher in his friend's wedding.[5]

As far as we know, nothing unusual happened aboard the flight for the first forty-six minutes of the journey.[6] At 9:03 a.m., United Airlines Flight 175 hit the South Tower of the World Trade Center.[7] At 9:24 a.m., as Flight 93 flew from Pennsylvania into Ohio, a United Airlines dispatcher sent this message to sixteen airborne flights: "Beware any cockpit intrusion. Two aircraft hit World Trade Center."[8] At approximately 9:28, as Dahl sought confirmation for that message, the hijackers burst into the cockpit and "incapacitated" him and his co-pilot.[9] The plane was rerouted back towards the east coast at it passed over Cleveland.[10] The four attackers, the eldest of whom was twenty-six years old, then demanded that the passengers and remaining crew sit in the back of the plane and be quiet. Before 9/11, airlines trained their crews to submit to the demands of hijackers, who most often wanted planes to land safely so their material demands could be met.[11]

Between 9:30 and 10 a.m., thirteen passengers made thirty-seven phone calls—two from cell phones and the rest from the Airfones in the back of the aircraft.[12] Tom Burnett, one of the passengers, called his wife Deena, who told him about what had happened in New York City. Deena called 9-1-1 and eventually reported the hijacking to the FBI as she fielded four calls in total from Tom aboard Flight 93. As Mrs. Burnett and others relayed news from the ground concerning the World Trade Center and then the Pentagon, the passengers and crew aboard Flight 93 began to realize their plane was part of a larger mission. At one point, Deena told her husband to "just sit quietly" and avoid drawing attention to himself. "Deena!" Tom replied, "If they're going to crash this plane into the ground, we're going to have to do something."[13]

Indeed, minutes later, the passengers sealed Tom Burnett's assertion with a vote, according to a call passenger Jeremy Glick made to his wife Lyz. Tom Burnett said they intended to wait until the plane was over a rural area. "There are three other guys on board as big as I am," Glick told his wife, "and we're going to do something." "Go for it," Lyz replied. Meanwhile, Joe DeLuca called his father. Linda Gronlund left a message for her sister Elsa and told her of the hijacking and informed her of the location of her will and other important documents.[14] Lauren Grandcolas left a message for her husband on the couple's answering machine. At 9:37 a.m., American Airlines Flight 77—which had been a nonstop flight to Los Angeles—crashed into the Pentagon in Arlington, Virginia.[15]

At 9:55 a.m. on Flight 93, the autopilot was reprogrammed to Reagan National Airport in Washington, D.C. Sandra Bradshaw told her husband that some aboard the plane had begun boiling water to throw at the hijackers. At 9:58 a.m., the calls ended as the passengers and crew put their plan into action. Todd Beamer asked Airfone operator Lisa Jefferson if she thought the passengers should fight back. "I'm right behind you, Todd," she answered. Beamer then said a prayer and put the phone down as the passengers began implementing their plan. Jefferson heard him say, "Let's roll." Bradshaw, on the phone with her husband, said: "Everyone's running to first class. I've got to go. Bye!" CeeCee Lyles told her husband: "They're breaking into the cockpit!"[16]

The exact events that unfolded between 9:58 a.m. and 10:03 a.m. are unknown. Some of the struggle for control of the plane ("Go! In the cockpit. In the cockpit. If we don't we'll die.") was captured by the cockpit voice recorder. Also audible is the hijackers' response: "They want to get in here. Hold, hold from the inside. Hold from the inside."[17] Investigators were able to piece together much of what happened, though they will never know precisely who was doing what or what exactly happened during those five crucial minutes.

That tape was played during the sentencing trial of Zacarias Moussaoui. According to *Washington Post* writers Jerry Markon and Timothy Dwyer, "The thirty-two-minute tape recounts an epic struggle as passengers surged forward to retake the plane using whatever low-tech weapons they could find . . . Much of the tape is unintelligible. There was loud static, and the voices, some speaking in English and others Arabic, were often inaudible. It cannot be determined whether the passengers entered the cockpit, although it is certain they came close and forced the hijackers to abandon their attack on Washington."[18]

Allah akbar!
Allah akbar!
Allah akbar!
Allah akbar!
Allah akbar!
Allah akbar!
Allah akbar!
Allah akbar!
Allah akbar![19]

Allah is the greatest!" the terrorists are heard to scream as they plunge to their death. The courtroom, according to the *Post* report, responded to the tape's eerie final silence with a profound quiet of its own.[20]

At 9:58 a.m., the plane was so low that a passenger named Edward Felt successfully called a Westmoreland County, Pennsylvania 9-1-1 dispatch center from his cell phone. He was able to report that United Flight 93 had been hijacked heading from Newark to San Francisco. He passed along his name and phone number to the 9-1-1 dispatcher, as well as the observation that the flight was "pretty empty."[21]

On the ground, Pennsylvanians in a neighboring county saw the plane's wings tipping from side to side. It is believed that the hijackers were intentionally manipulating the aircraft to disrupt the passengers' and crew members' plans. Residents of a nearby town named Lambertsville said Flight 93 looked like it was barely clearing the trees. In a scrap yard on Skyline Road near Lambertsville, workers said the plane was only forty or fifty feet off the ground when it passed over them. It hit the ground at 563 miles per hour with 7,000 gallons of jet fuel in its tank—a collision that produced a violent explosion and a ball of fire that rose above the local tree line. The plane's impact created a crater estimated to be about fifteen feet deep and thirty feet wide.[22]

When it crashed in Somerset County, Pennsylvania, at 10:03 a.m., Flight 93 was roughly twenty minutes—125 miles—from Washington, D.C.[23] It is believed that the U.S. Capitol was the terrorists' intended target. There was a joint session of Congress scheduled on September 11, 2001—which means every member of Congress (along with their staff) was in the building.

Minutes after the crash, nine different emergency response teams arrived at what they knew from Felt's distress call was a crime scene—not an accident scene. A Pennsylvania state trooper identified burnt copies of United Airlines' in-flight magazines. The scene quieted as they realized there would be no survivors to save. Photographer Dave Lloyd, also a first responder, said: "They were doing a search in hopes of finding survivors. I know some of the people that I could see were very upset about it, because in a fire service, we always train to save lives. And just the look on a lot of the faces there, we know we couldn't save anybody. It was just real quiet."[24]

The search for additional evidence would continue for thirteen days. By its end, more than 1,500 people would contribute to the investigation. And still, only around 8 percent of the remains of those aboard Flight 93 were recoverable, which is why the actual crash site is today considered a cemetery. Search teams were able, however, to recover enough to positively identify everyone aboard the plane. On Thursday, September 13, the flight data recorder—which would unlock critical information regarding Flight 93's flight path, altitude and tilt in the moments leading up to the crash—was found buried more than 15 feet below the surface. The next day, investigators recovered the cockpit voice recorder. The tremendous force of the crash had driven it twenty-five feet deep.[25] The largest piece of wreckage salvaged from the site was merely six feet-by-seven feet.[26]

A temporary memorial would soon be constructed as thousands of visitors left heartfelt tokens—flags, poems, candles, flowers, cards and messages—to express the many emotions they experienced in this silent, windswept corner of Somerset County. As of February 2009, more than one million visitors had made their way to Shanksville, Pennsylvania, to pay their respects. A permanent memorial is planned to honor the extraordinary deeds of the passengers and crew of Flight 93. Centered on a tree-lined walkway leading down to the sacred ground of the crash site, the memorial will also feature forty groves of trees indigenous to the area. A 93-foot Tower of Voices housing forty wind chimes—representing the forty voices that were raised up against the four hijackers—will sound above the silence that has descended on this peaceful meadow since the crash.[27]

CHAPTER SIX

EMPOWERING INSTINCT

"Recommendation: Targeting travel is at least as powerful a weapon against terrorists as targeting their money."—9/11 Commission Report[1]

One way to target terrorists' travel would be to hunt them down. And President Bush, in the days immediately following September 11, 2001, promised to do as much: "We'll find those who did it," he famously promised from Camp David. "We'll smoke them out of their holes, we'll get them running, and we'll bring them to justice."[2] Roughly six weeks later, the United States invaded Afghanistan, launching a war that rages onward under a new president eight years later.

But it would seem that targeting al-Qaeda and Taliban travel would also involve sealing shut the gaping holes in U.S. security that nineteen al-Qaeda hijackers penetrated in the weeks leading up to (and including) September 11. The 9/11 Commission Report urged lawmakers in Congress and policymakers in the executive branch to "combine terrorist travel intelligence, operations, and law enforcement in a strategy to intercept terrorists, find terrorist travel facilitators, and constrain terrorist mobility."[3] Improvements upon so-called terrorist watch lists had been made, the commission acknowledged, but "new insights into terrorist travel" still needed to be brought to the front lines of U.S. border security—which the commission recommended include "a larger network of screening points that includes our transportation system and access to vital facilities, such as nuclear reactors."[4] Border security officials needed to be trained to recognize fraudulent documents and work closer with intelligence agencies to keep track of the travelers carrying them. To do so, information and analysis programs had to be expanded and made more accessible ("Information systems able to authenticate travel documents and detect potential terrorist indicators should be used at consulates, at primary border inspection lines, in immigration services offices, and in intelligence and enforcement units. All frontline personnel should receive some training").[5] And a traveler screening system should be perfected and disseminated throughout border security agencies to ensure that U.S. officials working the front lines "have the tools and resources to establish that people are who they say they are, intercept identifiable suspects, and disrupt terrorist operations."[6]

The man in charge of this overhaul was Robert C. Bonner, the first commissioner of U.S. Customs and Border Protection (CBP)—the agency created by the Department of Homeland Security to manage and control the nation's borders in a post–9/11 world. At a basic level, that effort, Commissioner Bonner said in an interview, amounted to implementing the strategies used by frontline-inspectors like Jose Melendez-Perez and Diana Dean. By "asking questions, reading behavior, and using their border authority," the two had effectively rebuffed al-Qaeda-trained operatives in their plots to kill innocent people, the commissioner said.[7] Customs and Border Protection was able to design policies and practices for terrorist screening, Bonner said, by empowering their inspectors with "the authority of the border agency to deny entry," as well as "a system whereby you can identify individuals based upon strategic intelligence—not only what they look like—about where they're from and their travel patterns and the like." Added to that of course was training in how to conduct interviews and perform "behavioral reads as to the truthfulness" of a person's responses.[8] Those evaluations were being performed by border inspectors better informed by critical, up-to-the minute data from flight manifests and passenger name records, the commissioner stated.

In short, he continued, "There is now an evaluation of every person, for the first time, for potential terrorist risk." In other words, all visitors became subject to counterterrorism questioning similar to the methods Melendez-Perez employed during his confrontation with Mohamed al-Kahtani.[9] "The fact is that the basic model for this is what Jose Melendez-Perez did on August 4, 2001." He continued: "What he did was exceptionally courageous, and the reason is that the primary mission of INS before 9/11 was not keeping terrorists out—it was keeping economic migrants out."[10]

Indeed, before the attacks of September 11, Commissioner Bonner noted, the reality was that INS wasn't looking for terrorists. As Jayson P. Ahern, the assistant commissioner for field operations of CBP (who eventually served as CBP's acting commissioner), recalled in an interview, the traditional mission of customs pre–9/11 involved drug smuggling, interdiction, and money-laundering investigations.[11] But the Homeland Security Act, passed in 2002 and made effective in March 2003, abolished INS and gave the newly formed CBP the task of preventing terrorists and their potential weapons from getting into the United States. So when Commissioner Bonner took the helm, he first had to empower frontline Customs and Border Protection inspectors like Melendez-Perez to carry out this new mission. That overhaul required teaching and authorizing field officers to use interrogation tactics to "identify individuals who are not believable and who pose a potential terrorist threat." That would take not just instinct, he said, but ultimately a combination of "instinct and training and empowerment."[12]

The transition, he explained, entailed more than simply briefing border inspectors on their new agency and updated mission. "We've also got to be trained in behavioral reads and characteristics and engage in counterterrorism questioning for those relatively few individuals who are presenting a significant number of terrorist risk factors." He expressed confidence that CBP was fulfilling its critical mission: "We're just not letting [those] people into the United States anymore."[13]

That meant changing the agency culture that fostered sentiments like those expressed by Melendez-Perez's coworker ("Are you crazy, two Saudis in less than a week? This will get you in trouble!") after Melendez-Perez denied a second politically sensitive traveler in August of 2001. In other words, CBP needed to support personnel who made a determination that a traveler attempting to enter the U.S. was not believable or potentially dangerous. Post–9/11 frontline CBP officers and supervisors are encouraged to deny entry to any individual "if there is any risk to the safety and security of America by letting somebody in," Commissioner Bonner said. CBP has added to this new policy what the commissioner called a "method to identify individuals who pose possible terrorist risks so that they all receive counterterrorism questioning but without the burdens that [Melendez-Perez] faced."[14]

Bottom line: after going through the interrogation process with an individual, if an inspector has reason to believe the visitor is exhibiting definite terrorist risk factors, that inspector is now instructed to deny admission. "That is now the standing policy of Customs and Border Protection as part of the Department of Homeland Security, and that has as much to do with the fact that there hasn't been another terrorist attack in the United States since 9/11 as anything we've done," Commissioner Bonner said.[15]

As proof of this, he pointed to the fact that Customs and Border Protection denied admission to "about four-hundred to five-hundred people a year" who have exhibited multiple terrorist risk factors or whose stated intentions for entering the United States have been deemed not credible.[16] Admittedly, he said, we "don't know how many of those four-hundred or five-hundred individuals whom we've denied entry are in fact terrorists."[17] But to clearly illustrate the kinds of people CBP denied due to violated risk factors, Commissioner Bonner told the story of Ra'ed Mansour al-Banna. On February 28, 2005, Banna blew himself up near a health clinic in the Iraqi town of al-Hilla—killing 132 people and injuring 120 more. It was the worst suicide bomb attack in Iraq up to that time. Yet the part of the story rarely told is that Banna, a Jordanian citizen, had attempted to enter the United States less than two years before his suicide mission. Flying from Jordan to Chicago's O'Hare International Airport (after a layover in Amsterdam), Banna was denied entry when, according to Commissioner Bonner, he displayed at least four terrorist risk factors to the border inspectors who were screening him. These red flags were raised even though Banna had previously lived in the United States for nearly two years and supposedly "loved life in America, compared to Arab countries."[18] The CBP officer who conducted secondary screening with Banna determined that he was "not believable about his purpose for entering the country."[19] She did not know, the commissioner noted, that he was a terrorist (and indeed, Banna had previously exhibited all indications of having been Westernized). After being denied entry to the United States, Banna returned to Jordan, where he "became withdrawn, holing up in a makeshift studio apartment, sleeping late, and displaying a new interest in religion. He began praying five times a day and listening to the Koran. In November 2004, he went on pilgrimage to Mecca, returning to Saudi Arabia in January 2005."[20] The following month, he drove a truck loaded with improvised explosives into a health clinic in Iraq, killing himself and 132 innocent Iraqis.

How do we know that it was Banna who drove the truck that killed so many people? As it turns out, Iraqi investigators recovered his hand (that was all that was left of him) from the vehicle. It had been handcuffed to the steering wheel. When the hand was turned over to the U.S. military, it was discovered that his fingerprints matched those obtained by CBP inspectors when they refused to admit him into the U.S.[21] According to Commissioner Bonner, it wasn't quite an instinct that Banna was going to do harm that led CBP inspectors to become suspicious. It was more that their training led them to conclude that his story was not believable— and the fact that, in a post–September 11 world, CBP officers were then required to deny entry to those whose behavior, background, or travel patterns suggested that they posed a possible risk.[22]

Ahern, the assistant commissioner for field operations of CBP, was among those in charge of actually implementing this significant policy shift. His job was to oversee roughly twenty-five thousand men and women who guard more than three-hundred front-line ports of entry around the country and overseas—a position he attained by working his way up through the ranks after beginning as a customs inspector. Prior to his appointment as assistant commissioner, Ahern was the field manager of operations in San Diego as well as a port director in Los Angeles and Miami.[23] In other words, this was a guy who had earned his stripes along the front lines of border security.

Commissioner Ahern implemented a twofold approach to training border agents to effectively recognize potential terrorists seeking access to the United States. First, the CBP created counterterrorism response teams headed by agency personnel experienced in interviewing and investigation. Second, the agency turned to the private sector to hire experts in what's called "detecting deception and eliciting response" to train CBP inspectors on the kinds of tactics that Melendez-Perez knew implicitly and implemented instinctively. Instinct, Commissioner Ahern said, "can be taught to a degree." He added: "A lot of people have it, but not everyone."[24]

Regardless, the training is important because inspectors face an extraordinarily difficult task in trying to ferret out would-be terrorists, he noted. Whereas a drug smuggler or person traveling with forged documents is often clearly in violation of the law, Ahern pointed out that a potential terrorist may very well have a clean record with no tangible evidence pointing to his true intentions (Kahtani himself is a perfect example of this). The astute inspector therefore must be on the lookout for ways in which the suspected person's "purpose and intent do not add up," or for "links to associates who are known to be involved in terrorist activities."[25] When these emerge, the inspector must use his or her authority to deny entry.

How often were such individuals actually turned away? According to Commissioner Ahern, in fiscal year 2005, CBP prevented 493 individuals from entering the country based on "potential terrorist or security concerns." In fiscal year 2006, that number was 435.[26] Not all of those instances had terrorist watch lists to support a border inspector's intuitive perceptions and interrogation skills. Admittedly, they also amount to only a small percentage of the more than half a million people that are annually denied entry. And they certainly do not have the dramatic ending of the Kahtani or Banna stories—pursuit in the caves of Tora Bora or a mangled hand strapped to a steering wheel in Baghdad.

They are, however, highly significant to Commissioner Ahern because they represent the "most critical category" cases, which is more than enough reason for him to stress to his field agents the need to use their post–9/11 authority to deny entry in cases where there is "the slightest reasonable suspicion" of a visitor's true purpose and intention.[27] Why? Because every single one of those four- to five-hundred persons might be the next Mohamed Atta or Mohamed al-Kahtani—sent to the U.S. to carry out a mission or simply to probe and pry at our border security systems and protocols in preparation for the next big attack.

So how to identify the jihadist needle in the immigration haystack? That's a question for Barry McManus, whose resume includes more than three decades of experience in behavioral assessment, interviewing, and information elicitation. After serving as a detective with the Washington, D.C., Metropolitan Police Department, McManus worked as a polygraph examiner and interrogator with the CIA for more than twenty years, including ten years as the agency's chief polygraph examiner. That experience pitted his skills and knowledge directly against potential terrorists, hostile intelligence services, and other high-threat targets. He has traveled to more than 130 countries and extensively studied terrorism in the Middle East, Africa, Asia, Europe, and Latin America. Numerous government training programs and scholarly articles, including publications by the Department of Defense Polygraph Institute (DODPI) and the *American Polygraph Association Journal,* have resulted from the comprehensive research he has conducted on the polygraph as well as in the field of interviewing and elicitation strategies. Since September 2003, he has been working in the civilian sector as vice president of deception detection services for Abraxas Corporation, an overseas business intelligence and consultancy company.

McManus believes that deception detection is only the first step of the post–9/11 training regimen for government personnel. On the one hand, he said, an effective interrogator must master hard data, such as social indicators (age and physical appearance, for instance), cultural considerations (their manner of dress), and verbal and nonverbal physiological communication. But the next—and frankly, more difficult facet of interrogation training (unless a person has some kind of innate ability)—is teaching the art of eliciting information through indirect persuasion, or "convincing someone that you're a person that they want to talk to," as McManus describes it.[28] The two aspects of information elicitation are integral, and instinct can play a powerful role in both, McManus said. Asked, for example, if being "creeped out" by a terrorist in the manner of Jose Melendez-Perez is normal for interrogators, McManus responded that it was "atypical." He quickly added that having personally talked with a number of terrorists around the world, he believed that "when you walk in the room the first time you're faced with someone [like that] you instinctively perceive that something doesn't fit, something's not right about how they look and behave."[29]

That sense of the uncanny is crucial for phase two: information elicitation. As the interrogator begins to question the individual, he or she must try to establish normality, or rather what's normal for that person, "and then when something doesn't fit into that puzzle—that's your first indicator," McManus noted.[30] The abnormality is not usually a dead giveaway to the person's true purposes. But it is a clue, an indicator of potentially malicious intent—and a good interrogator must learn to recognize and to exploit it.

So instinct may give the interrogator the initial edge by allowing him or her a particular point at which to apply the science in which they've been trained. From there, McManus's job was to help his trainees learn what to do with "the tell" they had intuitively uncovered. In his words: "Barry McManus comes in and says, 'Ok, let's fine tune that intuitiveness you have—that instinct you have and everyone has.' As I like to say, people are more alike than different. Everyone has a little bit of the same DNA, and you just have to know the differences. So what I do is I come in and say, 'Ok, let's put the science to what you're looking at and what you're looking for. And after we put the science to it, let's talk about the art form.' "[31] McManus agreed that the "art form" involves the interrogator's God-given ability to detect when someone is not telling the truth—the BS-detector. People like Jose Melendez-Perez, he added, observe things instinctively based on years of experience. And that's key, he says, because the most important thing—"the thing that is going to save the United States from another 9/11 attack"—is information, or more specifically, our ability to elicit information from potential terrorists.[32]

Easier said than done, McManus noted in the same vein that Ahern did. After all, in most law-enforcement interrogation scenarios, the officer has leverage of some sort over the person being interviewed—drugs found in their possession, for example. But immigration inspectors and border personnel often lack that tangible leverage in the form of incriminating evidence. And moreover, McManus pointed out, the people they're interviewing may be highly trained operatives who have studied the protocols and procedures the inspector is using. Through systematic probing, he said, terrorist networks gradually and patiently learned what to expect when they arrive in the United States. In doing so, they lowered "the threshold of anxiety" that their operatives experienced when carrying out an actual terrorist plot. This process of probing, learning, and finessing counter-interrogation techniques takes place over a number of years, just as we saw with the planning of the attacks of September 11. So a border inspector must be aware of "all of the signs, the behavioral patterns, that a person may or may not give, based on what's deceptive and what's truthful, and then make a determination."[33] When the crucial element of time is factored in, according to McManus, the elicitor of information is placed in an extraordinarily difficult position. A highly trained terrorist operative can easily feed false information that an interrogator may not have time to properly evaluate.

In that regard, McManus urged his trainees to never forget one thing: Just as they are assessing the behavior and responses of their interviewee, they too are being observed—possibly by al-Qaeda-trained operatives who have some understanding of counter-interrogation techniques. "And they are motivated," he adds, "sometimes more so than we are, to clearly look for indicators [such as] how well trained you are, how well adept you are to asking the right questions, what behaviors you give away. It becomes a chess match with my wit versus his wit."[34]

Like Melendez-Perez, McManus can't help but give a critical once-over to the people he meets on a day-to-day basis. "After being in this business for as long as I have been, it becomes part of your fiber. It becomes part of who you are; sometimes it's good, and also sometimes it's not so good because you become somewhat cynical from time to time, and that's not healthy. But if you're going to be good at this profession then, as you say, some people have that intuitiveness, that innate ability, that instinct, which, if you fine tune it, you have a very powerful person."[35]

And like Ahern, McManus, believes that counterterrorism street smarts are something not everybody possesses naturally. They can, however, be taught, improved, and honed. Indeed, that is the objective of his training courses. "The mind," he insists, "is a very sensitive, delicate thing— more sensitive than the body. Inflicting pain can go away, but getting inside someone's head can do, sometimes, even worse damage."[36]

So what specifically were the techniques McManus and others were teaching U.S. border personnel? A December 2005 USA Today story, "Suspects' body language can blow their cover," reported, for example, that the federal government intended to "train screeners at forty airports in behavior analysis." These trainees would "join a growing number of police officers learning to detect the subtle, often unspoken clues that terrorists and criminals could display. The technique is called behavior detection or behavior-pattern recognition."[37]

The science behind it? The notion that people's speech patterns, facial expressions and responses to simple, straightforward questions are all embedded with subconscious clues to deeper thoughts, emotions and intentions.

Take for example the observations of Carl Maccario, a Transportation Security Administration (TSA) program analyst at Boston's Logan International Airport, about a tape of three September 11 hijackers going through security at Dulles International Airport. None of them, he noted, looked at the security guards. "They all looked away and had their heads down," Maccario said. "The fear of discovery changes people's behavior and body language."[38] Consider too the observations of Rafi Ron, the former head of security at Israel's Ben Gurion Airport, who stated, "Careful observation and questions of escalating intensity can unmask possible terrorists, who typically become anxious and deceptive around authorities." The founder of New Age Security Solutions, a private security business he based in Virginia and started in the weeks following September 11, Ron said: "There needs to be a shift in law enforcement culture from being responsive to criminal situations to being preventative by detecting the possibility of a terrorist attack."[39]

Fittingly, that's an attitude not unlike what the *Los Angeles Times* has called the "secret to thwarting terrorism" that has rightly earned Israel's El Al airlines the widespread reputation of being the safest airline in the world to fly. That is, the willingness to properly and thoroughly observe and interrogate travelers in the airport.[40] One passenger flying to Tel Aviv on business, the *Times* noted, was asked not only about his family and when he learned to speak Hebrew, but also, "On Passover, how many cups of wine do you drink?"[41] Indeed, Ann Davis, a TSA spokesperson at Boston's Logan

International Airport told the paper that the TSA's SPOT (Screening Passengers by Observation Technique) program "is a derivative of a program by the Israelis." Under the initiative, Davis explained, uniformed officers stationed near checkpoints would monitor incoming travelers for "involuntary physical and psychological reactions" that would supposedly indicate potential unease or deception. Screeners, she added, also "may engage the passenger in casual conversation to observe the response" and if they deem it necessary, send that person to be questioned further by police or airport officials.[42]

Another telling behavioral cue, according to psychologist and author Paul Ekman, who has long called for the government to study behavior in places like airports, includes the person "thinking really hard to answer a question they should know the answer to."[43] "Lab studies have proven people can detect liars," Ekman said. "We need studies to see if training can help people in the field."[44] Yet the real evidence does exist. Just ask Jose Melendez-Perez or Diana Dean.

The *USA Today* article also highlighted a story from the University of Maryland that illustrated how simple conversation could be used to uncover potentially criminal behavior. About a third of their campus police officers at the main campus near Washington, D.C., were trained to "help identify individuals that might pose some threat." Major Cathy Atwell from campus police said that subsequent to that training, "a university officer . . . got in a residence-hall elevator and noticed a man move to the back, stuff his hands in his pockets and not respond when the officer said hello. A conversation led to the man being charged with drug possession."[45]

A second *USA Today* article published at the end of 2005 described TSA plans to train screeners at forty major U.S. airports to proactively engage travelers in such conversations. The goal? To look for those who stumble or evade their way through that casual conversation and potentially subject those travelers to advanced screening or even police questioning.[46] On August 4, 2001, Jose Melendez-Perez's gut told him that something was amiss about the young Saudi trying to gain entrance to the United States. Melendez-Perez followed through on his instinctual feelings using a simple technique that he learned both as an Army recruiter and as an immigration inspector—he let his interviewee talk. And as Kahtani did so, Melendez-Perez listened carefully to his story and picked it apart. The TSA simply intended to take that conversation out of the screening room and into the airports and terminals in cities like New York, Los Angeles, Chicago, Houston, Detroit and Miami.[47] And they were not alone; other agencies training their personnel in behavior detection included airport police in Boston, Dallas/Ft. Worth, and Minneapolis–St. Paul; transit authorities in New York City and Washington, D.C.; U.S. Park Service police at the Statue of Liberty; and the NYPD Counterterrorism Bureau.[48] As Alvy Dodson, Public Safety Director at Dallas/Fort Worth International Airport, told *USA Today*'s Thomas Frank: "I don't want [officers] just sitting there waiting for a call to come in. I want them observing people, observing their behavior and engaging them in conversation. They're looking for people whose activities don't look right."[49] Having adopted this proactive attitude, nearly all of the airport police at Dallas/Fort Worth had been trained in the same techniques that allowed Melendez-Perez to stop the would-be twentieth hijacker.

It all amounted to a movement to take a closer look at passengers rather than just their luggage—"to become less obsessed with scissors and cigarette lighters and focusing more on passenger behavior," according to a May 17, 2006, piece in *Time Magazine*.[50] TSA officials, the piece reported, would be trained to recognize "unusual or anxious behavior" exhibited by travelers—things like sweating on a cold day or changes in voice pitch. Once again, local police would be on hand to question potentially dangerous passengers or run their names through criminal databases if necessary. The program, the piece noted, was not racially based and was, like most of the controversial post–9/11 security and interrogation techniques, implemented under a supervisor's watchful eye. "This system is conducted by trained personnel and closely monitored by supervisors," TSA Federal Security Director George Naccara said. "It provides another significant layer of security."[51]

In certain circumstances, of course, it makes sense to look for the bombs themselves (or bomb-making materials), especially when the devices can emit nuclear radiation or a chemical odor that may signal their presence and alert security personnel. Here, too, Customs and Border Protection seemed to be making progress. According to the CBP Web site, inspectors received advanced training on what were termed Weapons of Mass Effect (WME) such as biological, chemical, or nuclear bombs. WME Awareness Training "describes characteristics, tactics and strategies of terrorists, indicators of nuclear/radiological smuggling, characteristics of biological/chemical agents, as well as how terrorists are currently funding their activities, and how they can be detected in a trade-rich environment. In addition, the course identifies conventional explosives and their components, as well as pre-attack indicators."[52] The course also taught inspectors to look for rare materials "needed for the production of nuclear, chemical, and biological weapons and missile delivery systems." In a more advanced course taught by Department of Energy instructors and involving many practical exercises, CBP trainees learn the "descriptions of biological, chemical, nuclear and radiological devices/materials used in weapons of mass destruction."[53] The purpose of these new changes in the CBP training curriculum was to ensure that the field officer will know immediately what to do if they encounter a weapon of mass destruction/effect—or any component materials that could be used to create such a device.[54]

But what if we could spot the would-be terrorist long before he begins to build a bomb or hijack a plane—perhaps even before he first conceives of his plot? A February 2007 story in the *Guardian* reported: "A team of world-leading neuroscientists has developed a powerful technique that allows them to look deep inside a person's brain and read their intentions before they act. The research breaks controversial new ground in scientists' ability to probe people's minds and eavesdrop on their thoughts."[55] Though the actual study was an exercise in the infancy of reading people's intentions— the researchers were simply predicting whether the subjects planned to add or subtract two numbers shown to them—the implications of how the technique employed could be used in the future clearly had experts buzzing. The team, according to the *Guardian* piece, had learned to observe patterns of brain activity and translate them into "meaningful thoughts" that could be used to interpret "what a person planned to do in the near future."[56] "Using the scanner, we could look around the brain for this information and read out something that from the outside there's no way you could possibly tell is in there. It's like shining a torch around, looking for writing on a wall," said John-Dylan Haynes, who spearheaded the study from the Max Planck Institute for Human Cognitive and Brain Sciences in Germany.[57] Though the accuracy of the software that these scientists had developed was reportedly a commendable 70 percent, Professor Colin Blakemore, a neuroscientist and director of the Medical Research Council warned, "We shouldn't go overboard about the power of these techniques at the moment, but what you can be absolutely sure of is that these will continue to roll out and we will have more and more ability to probe people's intentions, minds, background thoughts, hopes and emotions."[58] The immediate and more benign application of the technology would be to develop brain-controlled computers and machinery "to boost the quality of life for disabled people."[59] And indeed, Honda unveiled similarly stunning technology in March of 2009 when the company demonstrated how a robot could be remote-controlled by the thoughts of a person wearing an elaborate and cumbersome electronic helmet.[60]

Similarly, the work of a criminologist at the University of Pennsylvania resulted in "a computer model for 'forecasting murder'" that Philadelphia's overworked and underfunded probation department would be able to access. A specialist in criminal statistics, Professor Richard Berk reported that he and a team of colleagues had developed software that produces a sort of criminality score by examining dozens of factors. "You can imagine the indicators that might incline someone toward violence: youth, having committed a serious crime at an early age, being a man rather than a woman, and so on. Each, by itself, probably isn't going to make a person pull the trigger. But put them all together and you've got a perfect storm of forces for violence," he said.[61] For example, a thirty-something first-time offender convicted of pistol-whipping would be less significant than if the perpetrator were eighteen years old, Berk explained.[62] Applied to the war on terror, Berk's software might enable us to anticipate tomorrow's terrorist today. Border security personnel like Melendez-Perez would have hard science to reinforce what their gut is telling them about a traveler who is behaving suspiciously.

So could the country embrace technological breakthroughs like Professor Berk's crime forecaster or brain-scan devices used to detect criminal intent? Media reports suggest that some would be resistant to the idea. According to the United Press International, some politicians have expressed serious doubts about a computer system already in place that screens travelers for "potential terrorist activity"—the Automated Targeting System (ATS-P). In 2007, according to a UPI story, Congressman Bennie Thompson (D-Mississippi) registered a range of objections to the system, "including the way it makes the travel records of U.S. citizens available to other government agencies."[63] Congressman Thompson, according to the UPI report, believed that CBP had created a "warrantless well of evidence from which any law enforcement, regulatory, or intelligence agency could dip at will—without any probable cause, reasonable suspicion, or judicial oversight."[64]

"'Without adequate safeguards,' he added, routine sharing of the information collected from Americans entering the country 'may constitute violations of the U.S. Constitution's Fourth Amendment guarantee against unreasonable searches and seizures.'"[65]

The broader criticisms of the post–9/11 behavior detection and airport security tactics follow a similar vein. When

Boston's Logan International Airport tried to be the first to implement the program of engaging travelers in casual conversation at airport checkpoints in 2002, the effort was challenged after an African American ACLU official said he was questioned and threatened with arrest if he didn't show identification. "If you're going to allow police to make searches, question people and even make arrests based on criteria rather than actual evidence of criminality, you're going to have racial profiling," American Civil Liberty Union's Barry Steinhardt reportedly said.[66] Massachusetts State Police Sgt. Peter DiDomenica disagreed. He called the program "an antidote to racial profiling" that—far from enabling the worst of investigators' personal biases—centered on "objective behavioral characteristics" in a way that discouraged racial profiling because it served to "educate people." Kelly Klundt of U.S. Customs and Border Protection had this to say: "U.S. Customs officers have long asked arriving travelers questions, often in random order. If a person gives 'stumbling answers,' that could indicate the person has fraudulent travel documents or plans to overstay a visa . . ."[67]

The controversy, of course, isn't restricted to Logan Airport. These new systems are being discussed nationally, especially with regard to their potential for misuse. Critics of behavior-based observational approaches believe that the potential for abuse outweighs the intelligence-gathering opportunities they offer. The ACLU, for instance, has repeatedly expressed a belief that studying people's actions or emotions might become proxy policy for targeting minorities. "When we begin to say to police officers that they're allowed to guess about who's dangerous, we're inviting the possibility of abuse," Steinhardt, director of the ACLU's technology and liberty program, reportedly told USA Today.[68] Jonathan

Turley of George Washington University Law School added that while so-called behavior detection is "a recognized and legitimate law enforcement tool . . . it's also ripe for abuse. A person's observations are often colored by one's bias and prejudices." Turley cited data from studies purporting to show how white people are more likely to glimpse a photo of a minority and "say the depicted minorities appeared dangerous . . . while minorities viewed fellow minorities as nonthreatening." The problem isn't police or security searches based on "reasonable suspicion" or criminal behavior or intent. It's that authorities should need more than a hunch fueling it, he said, noting that behavior-based interrogation techniques "can be used as a virtual script for the abusive officer. It gives a ready-made list of elements that can be claimed as reasonable suspicion."[69]

The 9/11 Commission, however, took a different view when it made its recommendations on how to prevent another terrorist attack against the United States. The Commission firmly and repeatedly advocated in support of the Customs and Border Protection agency's implementation of ATS-P. In particular, it highlighted the fact that prior to 9/11 "no agency of the U.S. government systematically analyzed terrorists' travel strategies" and that, "had they done so, they could have discovered the ways in which the terrorist predecessors to al-Qaeda had been systematically but detectably exploiting weaknesses in our border security since the early 1990s."[70]

Having been briefed by senior Customs and Border Protection's officials, the 9/11 Commission members made it clear with these recommendations that they were both familiar with the ATS-P initiative and were strongly advocating its heightened implementation.[71] In their own words, "a modern border and immigration system should combine a biometric entry-exit system with accessible files on visitors and immigrants, along with intelligence on indicators of terrorist travel."[72]

Brian Goebel is a former counselor to Commissioner Bonner at Customs and Border Protection and a leading expert on ATS-P. After working for Commissioner Bonner from September 2001 to May 2004, Goebel then went on to found his own private border-security consulting firm, The Sentinel HS Group, LLC. Goebel explained the "two primary sources of data that are used" by the ATS-P system. The first—passport and visa data—includes information gleaned from the documents themselves: name, date of birth, country of citizenship and gender, for instance. Meanwhile, Goebel continued, the U.S. government also maintained a separate system called the Passenger Name Record (PNR), which includes information such as how passengers purchased their tickets, seat location, how many bags were checked, and the length of the journey. "And those two sets of data are brought into the government computer system, if you will, and analyzed to look for exactly the kind of activities I was talking about at the beginning of the conversation: to look for passport and visa information that was lost, stolen, or fraudulent; to look for people who are on watch lists, not surprisingly; and also then to look for other indicators of potential terrorist or other security risks," Goebel said.[73]

The ATS-P system, he continued, represents the best of the federal security responses as prescribed by the 9/11 Commission: "They made several recommendations in the 9/11 Commission Report regarding the targeting of terrorist travelers, and three of them centered around the following," Goebel said. "First, the need to better identify false and fraudulent documents. One of the pieces of information that the government is currently collecting automatically is passport and visa data, so that they can do a better job of checking those passports and visas against databases of lost, stolen, or fraudulent passports and visas. So that's first."[74]

Second, Goebel continued, the Commission urged the government to more effectively provide what he called "tactical information—that is, specific information about terrorists" to the frontline border inspectors expected to catch each potentially dangerous person attempting to enter the country. "That was one of the main problems, quite frankly, of 9/11," Goebel said. "Two of the nineteen were watch-listed but the process was so slow that they weren't found before they entered the United States. So, the system in place today allows us to use that information, immediately put it into a system, and essentially presort the hundreds of thousands of people who fly into the country every day to look for those who might actually pose a risk."[75]

And finally, as for the potential malafides not on the terror watch lists—and "most of the nineteen were not," Goebel noted—the 9/11 Commission recommended that the country improve its ability to spot and assess "terrorist indicators." "Using that information that we know about terrorist behavior (motives, modus operandi, and the like), we can put a system in place—an 'information system' as the 9/11 Commission calls it—to allow our frontline border inspectors to identify those terrorists before they enter the United States. That's exactly what U.S. Customs and Border Protection has done."[76]

So keeping in mind Jose Melendez-Perez's encounter with Mohamed al-Kahtani, what if, by way of example, one passenger is traveling from Norway—his country of origin, of birth, and of citizenship—and another is from Saudi

Arabia? Is this system going to assign a higher terror risk level to the Saudi national? That information alone, Goebel said, wouldn't be sufficient to form an accurate risk analysis. But the combination of a broader set of factors—information that suggested "that a group of terrorists would be traveling on a certain category of passports, or certain passport set, with certain types of visas, and that they would be male, and perhaps in a certain age range," for example—would prescribe that any traveler (or group of travelers) meeting that criteria would be predetermined as worthy for additional interrogation. "So the system certainly makes some judgments and passport is certainly a factor, but it wouldn't do it solely on that basis alone," Goebel explained.[77]

In fact, he continued, that reality served to guard against ATS-P devolving into a tool for unwarranted racial profiling of, in this case, Saudis or Middle Eastern men in general. For one thing, Goebel noted, U.S. border inspectors and checkpoints don't have the ability to inspect that many travelers. "And we know from practical experience that not every Saudi poses a threat to the United States. Not every person from the Middle East in general poses a threat to the United States. I don't want to dance around this too much; I just want to say that the system takes all relative factors into account, and certainly citizenship, travel patterns, travel country, indicia of resemblance to other terrorists that we've seen before—all of those factors are brought to bear in the system. But the output of the system allows our inspectors to make much more educated decisions about those persons whom they might need to spend more time with."[78]

"And I just want to point out that the system works—something that hasn't been discussed very well in the media so far. Every day, the U.S. government, my old agency,

Customs and Border Protection, identifies hundreds if not thousands of fraudulent and false travel documents and they return—that is, deny admissibility—to dozens if not hundreds of people who are trying to get in to the United States and whom we have determined are not lawfully trying to enter. Many of those people are security threats."[79]

The common misconception, Goebel continued, is the notion that every traveler is assigned a personal score or risk number that permanently blacklists them any time they want to go somewhere. That perception, however, is based on the confusion people have in distinguishing between cargo screening systems—which do in fact assign numerical scores—and the passenger evaluation system. When assessing passengers, Goebel explained, the system doesn't assign a specific "risk score" to that person. Rather, he said, it points out specific terror indicators which the traveler has violated—leaving the border inspector and interrogators to assess those red flags and determine whether a person is fit to be admitted to the country. It isn't, Goebel, said, "a system where the computer just decides your fate. That's not how the government works. That's not how our borders work. Every person that comes into the country has an opportunity to—and is in fact legally required to—meet with a U.S. Customs and Border Protection officer so that person can make a decision as to whether to admit them into the United States. And so the system simply provides these officers—who are well trained and, I would point out, have caught terrorists in the past—with extra information that they can use to more quickly and effectively sort passengers and make decisions on who needs more time in an interview and who doesn't."[80]

He continued: "There's been a lot of discussion about how this system essentially blacklists people. And I want to point out that in this environment, it's actually completely the opposite, which is that you have an immediate opportunity for redress, which is something that the privacy community hasn't pointed out: if you're identified by the system as somebody who may pose a higher risk, you then have an opportunity—and in fact are required by law—to go talk to a customs officer. They make the final decision if you're a risk or not. And if you're not, that information is captured in the system and you're allowed to enter the United States. You're not perpetually blacklisted! You were looked at, and it was determined that you were not a threat."[81]

So the system looks at, broadly speaking, two categories of information: passport and visa data, which would include name, date of birth, citizenship, and so forth. And then it also looks at travel patterns and ticketing information. Does that mean that someone sitting in the first row of the plane in first class raises more red flags in the risk assessment databases? Choosing his words carefully, Goebel explained, "I don't want to say that they would be placed at higher risk, because I don't want to talk about how the system operates, but the system would be aware of that information and would make judgments based on those kinds of factors—like I said, it would include seating assignments, checked bags, how the ticket was bought, when it was bought, how long you're going to be traveling, what your 'legs' are—those kinds of issues are going to be looked at and analyzed by the system."[82]

What's clear is that even an advanced computer data system like ATS-P, which is designed to provide up-to-the-minute information to frontline CBP officers with the click of a button, is useless without the hard data that is fed into it. What is needed, therefore, is a standardized means of traveler identification and documentation—and the Department of Homeland Security's Western Hemisphere Travel Initiative (WHTI) fits that bill. Implemented in January of 2007 as a result of 9/11 Commission recommendations, the Western Hemisphere Travel Initiative closed possible loopholes in our border security by requiring that all air travelers reentering the United States from Canada, Mexico, and Bermuda carry their passport or one of a few other officially accepted documents. In June of 2009, the initiative expanded to include all travelers entering the United States by crossing borders—or those traveling by sea or air—to present a passport or another of the accepted forms of identification (such as a "trusted traveler" card or an enhanced drivers license).[83] In January of 2009, mere statements of nationality were no longer accepted as proof of origin at border checkpoints.[84]

Stories of terrorists like Ra'ed Mansour al-Banna trying to cross our borders after 9/11 exemplify that much work remains to be done not only to maintain but also to increase the level of our national vigilance. But it's clear that Jose Melendez-Perez has rightfully made a significant impact upon the policies of several federal agencies. That is a truly American story, and one that offers great hope for our country's future security and the safety and prosperity of our children as they face the ongoing threat of international terrorism in a world of suitcase nukes and biological weapons.

As Malcolm Gladwell observed in *Blink*, while our conversation with a total stranger remains probably the "most basic of human rituals," it nevertheless "turns out to be a minefield."[85]

Indeed, it does.

CHAPTER SEVEN
GITMO

For months after his arrival at the United States naval base at Guantanamo Bay, Cuba, nobody knew the identity of Detainee 063. He had been captured by Pakistani authorities on December 15, 2001, after attempting to retreat from Tora Bora, transferred to American custody on December 26, 2001, and shipped to Guantanamo on February 13, 2002.[1] He refused to cooperate with his interrogators. They suspected he was a Saudi, which he denied.[2] He repeatedly offered what the Department of Defense deemed "cover stories ranging from claims of being in Afghanistan to buy falcons to claims he was coming to the U.S. to buy a used car."[3]

Then, in July 2002, the FBI caught a break. They matched their mystery detainee's fingerprints to those of a Saudi "tourist" who'd been questioned at Orlando International Airport in August of 2001 and sent back to Dubai.

Mohamed al-Kahtani.

Digging further into the events that transpired as Jose Melendez-Perez interviewed Kahtani on August 4, 2001, FBI agents discovered that somebody had used a pay phone at the airport to call Mustafa al-Hawsawi, the al-Qaeda logistical coordinator then living in the United Arab Emirates. Surveillance cameras captured Mohamed Atta's rental car arriving at the airport around the time Kahtani's plane was scheduled to land.[4] Investigators concluded during the summer of 2002 that Kahtani was intended to be the fifth hijacker on United Airlines Flight 93—and the twentieth hijacker to participate in the September 11, 2001, attacks.[5]

The FBI was responsible for interrogating Kahtani between July 27, 2002, and September 19, 2002, a period the detainee split between Camp Delta and the Naval Brig at Guantanamo. It was during this time that Department of Defense officials began considering an enhanced interrogation plan aimed at intensifying Kahtani's questioning. In September of 2002, an official from the Department of Defense Criminal Investigative Task Force (CITF), created to assist in the investigation of detainees captured in the war on terror, expressed concerns about that developing plan. According to the CITF commander's memo, included in it was the intention to "drive the hooded detainee around the island to disorient him, disrobe him to his underwear, have an interrogator with an Egyptian accent (it is known among the detainees that Egyptians are aggressive interrogators and commonly use coercion, to include maiming)." The memo continued: "As a law enforcement agency, CITF is clearly prohibited from participating in these techniques and we also do not want to turn a deaf ear when we learn of these issues . . ."[6]

Those enhanced interrogation methods seem to have been introduced in the fall of 2002. The Associated Press in December of 2004 obtained a letter written by a senior Justice Department official that alleged "highly aggressive interrogation techniques" were employed with several detainees at the U.S. naval base in 2002.[7] In one case cited in the letter, the FBI official reported that interrogators had used a dog "in an aggressive manner to intimidate" a detainee in September or October of 2002. In November, the letter continued, the same detainee—after being subjected "to intense isolation for over three months" in a cell "always flooded with light"—was displaying behavior consistent with "extreme psychological trauma" such as "talking to nonexistent people, reporting hearing voices, crouching in a cell covered with a sheet for hours on end."[8] Subsequent reportage by *Time Magazine* would reveal that detainee to be Kahtani.

Between October 2, 2002, and October 10, 2002, a Guantanamo-based task force led Kahtani's interrogation—which then included, according to an FBI memo composed on October 8, 2002, sleep deprivation, loud music, bright lights, and "body placement discomfort, all with negative results." After those enhanced techniques resulted in a standstill, Kahtani was returned to the Naval Brig.[9] Worth noting with regards to the investigation into Kahtani's interrogation is that in November of 2002, Major General Geoffrey Miller became Commander at Guantanamo. Upon his arrival, Miller noted that there was "significant tension" between the Guantanamo task force, CITF and FBI officials as they sought common ground on an interrogation plan for Detainee 063.[10] That plan would become the first "Special Interrogation Plan" to emerge from Guantanamo—a fact that led one FBI special agent to believe it would set the tone for subsequent interrogations at the base "and therefore they 'had to get it right.'"[11]

A report of the U.S. Senate Armed Services Committee details two drafts of the updated Kahtani interrogation plan—one dated November 12, 2002, and the other dated November 22, 2002. The report indicates that there is evidence that Major General Miller approved both. With regards to the first memo, the stated purpose was to "break the detainee and establish his role in the attacks of September 11, 2001." According to an email sent by Diane Beaver, a staff judge advocate at Guantanamo, "concerning 63 [Kahtani], my understanding is that NSC [National Security Council] has weighed in and stated that intel on this guy is utmost matter of national security."[12]

The November 12 plan was fourfold. Phase I would be geared towards breaking Kahtani by not allowing him to speak. Phase II would include placing "a cooperative detainee or a native linguist at Camp X-Ray in full view of Khatani [sic]."[13] Phase III, submitted under the title "Level III techniques," included the implementation of techniques based on those used to train U.S. soldiers during Survival, Evasion, Resistance and Escape training—known for short as SERE training. SERE training, according to the Senate Armed Services Committee report, is designed to simulate for U.S. service members what tactics an enemy not operating under the Geneva Conventions might employ. In other words, SERE is intended to help U.S. personnel to resist divulging high-value information. Among those techniques, according to the report, were "stripping students of their clothing, placing them in stress positions, putting hoods over their heads, disrupting their sleep, treating them like animals, subjecting them to loud music and flashing lights, and exposing them to extreme temperatures."[14] Phase IV of the Kahtani plan, labeled "Coalition Exploitation," contained the following description: "The fourth phase of the plan to exploit 063 requires that he be sent off island either temporarily or permanently to either [two specific third world countries], or another country to allow those countries to employ interrogation techniques that will enable them to obtain requisite information."[15] The plan, however, was not implemented on November 15 as intended because Major General Miller requested more time to consider objections to the plan offered by CITF Commander Britt Mallow. On November 21, meanwhile, Major

General Miller participated in a video teleconference to discuss a compromise interrogation plan for Kahtani with officials from the FBI, CITF, SOUTHCOM and the Department of Defense's Office of General Counsel. The FBI emerged from that meeting expressing "misgivings about the overall coercive nature and possible illegality" of the interrogation plan, recommending in its place a more long-term effort based on rapport-building approaches.[16] Despite those objections, as well as those offered by Naval Criminal Investigative Service Chief Psychologist Michael Gelles ("... The choice to use force with this adversary in an interrogation may only reinforce his resistance . . ."), Major General Miller authorized the enhanced interrogation of Kahtani to proceed on November 23, 2002.[17]

The final plan for Kahtani's enhanced interrogation included five stages. During the first, Kahtani's interrogators would seek to establish an "isolated, austere environment" in which Kahtani would become entirely dependent on his inquisitors. U.S. interrogators would begin Phase II, largely the same as Phase I of the November 12 plan described above, by shaving Kahtani's head and beard. Phase III was mostly the same as Phase II of that earlier memo. Phase IV was also largely similar to that earlier plan, though the "final" approved plan contained this passage:

The fourth phase of the plan to exploit 063 requires [Office of the Secretary of Defense] approval for the SERE interrogation technique training and approval of the level three counter interrogation resistance training submitted by JTF-GITMO [Joint Task Force—Guantanamo]. Once the approvals are in place, those interrogation techniques will be implemented to encourage 063 to cooperate. The intent of raising the stakes to this level is to convince 063 that it is futile to resist. Success of Phase III is when his sense of futility is raised to a high enough level that source gives in and provides the necessary information. Phase III ends with success or a standstill, after the exhaustion of all tools JTF GTMO has to offer.[18]

The interrogation plan's final phase contained the same heading as the November 12 plan, but cut out specific reference to transferring Kahtani to another country. It stated: "The fifth phase of the plan to exploit 063 will be determined at the national, interagency level where the future disposition of 063 will be determined." The FBI, meanwhile, continued to express its skepticism. "Many of the methods are considered coercive by Federal Law Enforcement and UCMJ [Uniform Code of Military Justice] standards," read a November 22, 2002, memo sent to Major General Miller. "Not only this, but reports from those knowledgeable about the use of these coercive techniques are highly skeptical as to their effectiveness and reliability."[19] A CITF memo sent to Diane Beaver, meanwhile, advised that because CITF was "not on board" with the techniques planned for Kahtani, the organization's officials would "stand clear and not offer participation, advisements, support or recommendations as to its implementation."[20]

The question of what actually happened to Kahtani would be answered—at least in part—by a June 2005 exposé in *Time Magazine* titled "Inside the Interrogation of Detainee 063," which cited a secret log documenting his treatment in the weeks that followed. That time period also coincided with the decision to subject Kahtani to more intense interrogation techniques "personally authorized" by then-Secretary

Donald Rumsfeld, a related *Time* report indicated.[21] "Now the interrogators could use stress strategies like standing for prolonged periods, isolation for as long as thirty days, removal of clothing, forced shaving of facial hair, playing on 'individual phobias' (such as dogs) and 'mild, noninjurious physical contact such as grabbing, poking in the chest with the finger and light pushing,'" wrote Adam Zagorin and Michael Duffy.[22] Nearly nine months after publishing its exclusive story about Kahtani's detention, *Time* released the interrogation log that had precipitated it.

Mohamed al-Kahtani was a formidable adversary for U.S. interrogators, who throughout the fifty days documented in the log implemented several so-called "themes" and "approaches" into their sessions with the suspected twentieth hijacker. Each was designed to push their subject closer to revealing the details of his alleged terrorist ambitions and knowledge and further from his allegiance to al-Qaeda. At one point, the log notes, an interrogator used the analogy of an onion to explain to Kahtani how "control over his life is being stripped away" by his inquisitors. On November 26, 2002, the log states, an interrogator employed the "circumstantial evidence" theme—explaining to Kahtani that the known evidence of his crimes belied his cover stories. That same day, interrogators bombarded the prisoner with "harsh pride and ego down" routines, during which two interrogators staged a scripted discussion in Kahtani's presence. The aim was to peel away their detainee's sense of bravado and self-worth by implying that he was less than human (The discussion featured one questioner storming out of the room saying, "Human beings don't kill 3,000 people"). During another such approach in December, interrogators brought Kahtani outside and made him watch a family of banana rats. The rats, interrogators told him, exhibited more "love, freedom, and concern" than Kahtani could. The log notes that the detainee began crying.[23]

Kahtani's various responses to these different approaches were closely monitored and recorded in the eighty-four-page interrogation log. He often became physically confrontational with his captors. On November 25, 2002, interrogators began the day's shift as they often did by awakening Kahtani at four in the morning. After he did not respond to inquiries about God's mission and message for him, an interrogator leaned close to Kahtani's ear and asked, "What is God telling you right now? Your nineteen friends died in a fireball and you weren't with them. Was that God's choice? Is it God's will that you stay alive to tell us about his message?" At that point, Kahtani threw his head backwards and head-butted the interrogator in the eye. As guards wrestled him to the ground, Kahtani tried to spit at his interrogator, who stood over him and urged: "Go ahead and spit on me. It won't change anything. You're still here. I'm still talking to you and you won't leave until you've given God's message."[24]

That same day, medical personnel (who, according to the log, were on hand to check Kahtani's vital signs and his blood pressure several times a day) told interrogators that their subject needed to drink fluids or he'd be forced to receive them intravenously. When the IV was applied, Kahtani repeatedly reached to remove it, so guards handcuffed his hands to his chair. Kahtani then bent down and removed the IV by biting it in two. A new IV was applied soon thereafter, and Kahtani was fed an unknown amount of fluids. He soon complained that he had to urinate and offered to talk if interrogators would let him go to the bathroom. The conversation persisted:

Sergeant A: Who do you work for?
Kahtani: Al-Qaeda.
SGT A: Who was your leader?
Kahtani: Osama bin Laden
SGT A: Why did you go to Orlando?
Kahtani: I wasn't told the mission.
SGT A: Who was meeting you?
Kahtani: I don't know.
SGT A: Who was with you on the plane?
Kahtani: I was by myself.[25]

When Kahtani reiterated his desire to go to the bathroom, his interrogator told him: "You've ruined all trust, you can either go in the bottle or in your pants." So Kahtani urinated in his pants. Later that day, Kahtani would revert to claiming innocence, saying that he had admitted his affiliation with al-Qaeda because of the "intense psychological pressure" he was put under.[26]

The majority of the days included in the interrogation log look the same. Interrogators would awaken Kahtani at 4:00 a.m. and run a series of approaches and themes as a way of breaking him down. They would attempt to convince him of the futility of his resistance by discussing al-Qaeda's demise. Or the fact that other detainees were speaking with U.S. interrogators. Or by pointing out the inconsistencies in his cover story. They would tell him Osama bin Laden had hijacked Islam, and by cooperating with U.S. interrogators, Kahtani could redeem his religion. The interrogators were mostly met with silence, diversions, or the recounting of a cover story they believed not only false, but pulled straight out of an al-Qaeda instruction manual they said the terrorists had designed in part for situations just like the one Kahtani faced at Guantanamo.

On the evening of December 3, 2002—shortly after Secretary Rumsfeld approved the intensified questioning methods—the log notes that "Phase 1B" began. Kahtani was transferred to a new interrogation booth, one "decorated with photos of 9/11 victims, the U.S. flag, flags of coalition forces in the global war on terrorism, and red lighting."[27] That night, interrogators shaved his head and beard with electric clippers. Kahtani resisted, interrogators restrained him, and the shaving continued without incident once Kahtani proved compliant. "Photos were taken of detainee when the shaving was finished," the log noted. During the early hours of the next day, interrogators awakened Kahtani and began by mocking his cover story about being in Afghanistan to pursue falconry. They told him that Osama bin Laden was "making a whore of Islam."[28] Angered, Kahtani complained "about a picture of a 9-11 victim being taped to his trousers." Later that same day, Christina Aguilera music was blasted into his holding area.[29]

Kahtani himself shuffled through an array of diversionary tactics as his interrogators continued to apply their range of approaches. He told his captors "his emotions were making him behave badly, then started making odd faces." U.S. personnel answered that they "had seen crazy people before and he was not crazy," and their detainee stopped making the faces. Kahtani immediately attempted to reassert his own control by saying that "he was in charge now and they would bring him food and water when he wanted and they would let him sleep when he wanted." In response, Gitmo interrogators "established control over detainee by having him alternately sit and stand. Detainee seemed near crying and was told not to cry on this shift."[30]

As the interrogations entered this new phase, U.S. personnel continued ratcheting up new approaches in Kahtani's interrogation room. The "invasion of space by a female" tactic was among them—and one that elicited a particularly violent response. On December 5, 2002, the log indicates that Kahtani became "irritated" by a female officer hovering behind him and tried to push her away. He then spit at the two interrogators sitting in front of him "because he was annoyed by the female behind him." The next day, the log states, Kahtani again became "very violent and irate" during the "invasion of space" approach and tried to free himself from his chair—a struggle that lasted forty minutes—to get away from the female officer.[31]

That struggle, on December 6, 2002, came moments after the log records a small crack in Kahtani's resistance. On a day during which interrogators discussed Zacarias Moussaoui's capture, they told Kahtani that another detainee had identified Kahtani as being present at an al-Qaeda safe house, and employed an "al-Qaeda falling apart" theme. As a result, Detainee 063 told interrogators that he was ready to talk and "tell the truth." "I am doing this to get out of here," he said, though once he began talking, the log states, Kahtani would only discuss himself. "Detainee talked about traveling to Afghanistan and meeting UBL [Osama bin Laden] who gave him money and sent him to America. Detainee also talked about his travel after he was turned away from Orlando."[32]

One subplot throughout the interrogation log is the haggling with Kahtani about his food and fluid intake. From the first days recounted in the log, Kahtani insisted that he had undertaken a food and water strike. He would often recant and consume an MRE (Meal Ready to Eat) as medical personnel continuously checked his vital signs during those days when he refused to eat or drink. His consistent refusal to drink water would necessitate attaching an IV during interrogations. Late in the interrogation log, the medical staff on-hand for the interrogation gave Kahtani an enema as a way of combating dehydration.[33]

This medical haggling came to a head on December 7. At 8:00 p.m., a medical corpsman checked Kahtani's vital signs and found them to be unusually low. After a doctor performed an EKG scan and found his heartbeat to be just thirty-five beats per minute, Gitmo doctors elected to transfer Kahtani to the base hospital in order to perform a CT scan. At the hospital, doctors placed the detainee in an isolation ward, checked his electrolytes, examined his left leg for blood clots (none were found), and consulted a radiologist for any abnormalities in the CT scan. "The detainee slept most of the day between meals," the log noted on December 8, 2002.[34]

Kahtani was returned to his daily routine the following day. His interrogators showed him pictures of 9/11 victims, many of them children or elderly women ("SGT M asked the detainee what could these little old women do? Were they going to drop a bomb or fly a plane into the holy city of Mecca? The detainee shook his head and replied 'no.'").[35] They forced Kahtani to stand for the U.S. national anthem. They drowned out his attempts to reassert his cover story by screaming at him and playing loud music. When he dozed off during sessions, Guantanamo personnel dripped water on his head. The interrogation team brought up his past diversions, requesting, for example, that he "perform the 'crazy Mohammed' facial expressions again." When Kahtani began crying, his inquisitors "recounted the 'emotional Mohammed' from earlier in the session and the detainee became stoic again." As the December 16 sessions come to a close, the log notes: "He has not offered any new information. He's sticking to the same story. He came to the United States to buy used cars in order to sell them in Saudi Arabia or United Arab Emirates."[36] As the interrogations progressed, U.S. interrogators began introducing themes and approaches aimed at poking holes in that story. On December 18, the log notes: "Detainee states that he was involved in the auto business but he did not know much about the basic functions of an automobile. He knew that the battery provides a car with electricity in order to get it started. He did not know that the alternator recharges the battery after each time it is used to start the car. He would attempt to not understand the question in order to avoid answering the question about the alternator and other car parts. It should be noted that the detainee stated in an earlier session that he had run a car garage in Saudi Arabia for ten years."[37]

On December 21, the log indicates, Kahtani was strip-searched—a process he initially resisted. Soon, instead of defying his interrogators, he simply stared ("with GREAT focus") at the wall, embarrassed that female personnel were seeing him naked.[38] The following day, "Phase II" began with the introduction of what the log calls a "confederate detainee"—a U.S. interrogator posing as a fellow detainee in a sleep cell next to Kahtani's. This was a U.S. attempt to plant a "friendly" with whom Kahtani could forge a bond (and engage in a substantive conversation about his case). On December 24, interrogators woke Kahtani up in his cell just as a scripted operation involving that confederate detainee began. Guards and interrogators "appeared anxious that something was happening," and as Kahtani began to tremble, the nearby "detainee" attempted to calm him down. "Confederate asked the detainee 'what is your case' and detainee declared 'it is big' and began to cry."[39]

The "confederate" was phased out on January 2, 2003—little more than a week before the interrogation log ends—when an ambulance arrived, and he was informed "that the information he gave last night checked out, so the interrogators will keep their promise to send him to a better place to be with his cousins." As the undercover interrogator left his sleep cell carrying some fruit and a Koran, he yelled "God guide and direct you" in Arabic to Kahtani.[40]

Meanwhile, as the "confederate detainee" subplot played itself out in the background, U.S. interrogators planted the notion that things would get even worse for Kahtani if he refused to cooperate in the interrogation sessions. They hung pictures of "fitness models" around his neck and asked him questions as a means of measuring his ability and willingness to fully recount details when responding to interrogations. They instructed him to bark at pictures of terrorists. On December 24, the log indicates that Kahtani appeared near his breaking point: "Circumstantial evidence was the next theme used, the detainee was reminded that all the evidence shows that he is Al Qaida [sic] and that it is time to tell the truth, detainee sat there in silence for about a minute and seemed as he was going to let it all out, but stuck to his story again. The detainee is thinking a lot more on the themes when presented to him, seems to be on the verge of breaking."[41]

One such breakthrough occurred on the night of January 1, 2003. Kahtani had been given a reprieve from questioning for about twelve hours that day in his sleep cell, but he was still tired as the interrogator (identified as "2A0780") began a subtle line of questioning that led Kahtani to admit his affiliation with the 9/11 hijackers:

Detainee returned to the booth. 2A0780 entered the booth and began talking to detainee about what the Quran says about justice for orphans. 2A0780 ask detainee what made 19 young Saudi Arabian men want to kill themselves, detainee stated he was unsure, but maybe they were tricked. 2A0780 asked how could one man, Bin Laden, convince 19 young men to kill themselves, (detainee was starting to fade he was going in and out of sleep.) The question was repeated, detainee stated that they were tricked, that he distorted the picture if front of them, 2A0780 asked detainee if this made him mad, detainee stated yes, (detainee did not realize that 2A780 had now started putting detainee into the picture) 2A0780 asked detainee if he was mad that his friends had been tricked, detainee stated yes. 2A0780 asked detainee if his friends knew about the plan, detainee stated no, 2A0780 asked if detainee knew about the plan, detainee stated no, 2A0780 asked detainee if anyone knew about the plan, detainee stated yes. 2A0780 asked detainee if Mohamed Atta knew about the plan, detainee stated that he didn't know. 2A0780 asked detainee if it made him mad that he killed his friends, detainee stated yes. 2A0780 asked detainee if he was glad that he didn't die on the plane, detainee stated yes. 2A0780 asked detainee if his parents were happy that he didn't die detainee stated yes. 2A0780 stated "he killed your friends" detainee stated yes. 2A0780 asked detainee if his parents were happy that he wasn't on the plane, detainee stated yes. 2A0780 asked did you call your parents after you didn't get on the plane, detainee stated no. 2A0780 asked detainee you knew getting on the plane was wrong, detainee stated yes, 2A0780 then asked but you still wanted to fight, detainee stated yes. Detainee was having difficulty staying awake at this time. Detainee was becoming non responsive.[42]

According to the interrogation log, Kahtani's body language in the days after that exchange showed signs he was increasingly worried about the cover story he had provided, as well as his ability to continue to divert questioning. On January 2, he relented on a long-running point of contention with interrogators seeking information about his travels (with other members of al-Qaeda) after September 11: "Detainee was questioned about his trip from Mazar E Sharif to Kandahar with the use of a map. Detainee had previously denied ever being in Kabul but it was pointed out that he must have gone through Kabul to get to Kandahar. Detainee said that he had been through Kabul and apologized to interrogator. Interrogator awarded the detainee a respect point."

The next day, the log notes, "Interrogators asked if he would have gone to Orlando if he had known the mission. Detainee replied 'No'." The document's last entry comes at 7:00 a.m. on January 11, 2003. On January 15, 2003, Secretary Rumsfeld revoked his order to allow the harsh interrogation techniques he'd signed less than two months before.[43] Thereafter, Kahtani was transferred out of Camp X-Ray and encountered only Category I interrogation techniques (including "yelling and techniques of deception").[44]

At a Senate Armed Services Committee hearing in 2005, the Pentagon publicly declared that the so-called "harsh interrogation" had been a success—netting a confession from Kahtani as to his intended participation in the Flight 93 hijacking. "Air Force Lt. Gen. Randall M. Schmidt said that Mohamed al-Kahtani said he had expected to be aboard United Airlines Flight 93 . . . Schmidt said Kahtani confessed to participating in the hijacking only after frustrated interrogators began to use techniques that an FBI agent later complained were abusive," a Knight Ridder report indicated.[45] The Pentagon also publicly asserted that Detainee 063 had pointed the finger at thirty fellow detainees at Guantanamo he claimed were bin Laden bodyguards.[46]

Schmidt also told the Senate committee that his investigation of the FBI complaint led to the finding of two incidents of treatment that he considered excessive: once when Kahtani had been shackled to the floor and another occasion when "he was smeared with red ink that a female interrogator told him was menstrual blood."[47] Schmidt testified that "his investigation found that Kahtani was deprived of sleep, shackled to the floor on at least one occasion, interrogated for as many as twenty hours at a time, stripped naked and forced to endure extremes of heat and cold, all in an effort to get him to talk. He also said interrogators called Kahtani's mother and sisters whores, called him a homosexual, made him wear a woman's panties and a bra, forced him to dance with a male interrogator, put a leash around his neck and made him perform tricks like a dog," a report indicated at the time of the hearing. In other words, broadly speaking, the treatment of Kahtani conformed with the Army's 1987 interrogation manual or to more coercive techniques approved by the Secretary of Defense. Out of more than 24,000 interrogations, Schmidt told the Senate committee, he uncovered only three incidents of abuse—the two involving Kahtani and a third that "occurred when a Navy lieutenant commander threatened to kill an unnamed 'high-value' detainee and his family."[48]

Meanwhile, the Department of Defense insisted that the decision to enhance the interrogation of Kahtani was carefully considered and free of malice toward the al-Qaeda operative: "Kahtani's interrogation during this period was guided by a very detailed plan and conducted by trained professionals motivated by a desire to gain actionable intelligence, to include information that might prevent additional attacks on America," read a Department of Defense press release.[49] The department then contextualized Secretary Rumsfeld's decision to approve these enhanced interrogation techniques by citing the "post–9/11 environment" during the period those tactics were employed:

There had just been anthrax attacks in the U.S. in December of 2001.

Richard Reid tried to blow up a U.S. airliner with a shoe bomb.

Over the spring and summer, there were deadly attacks in Tunisia and Pakistan.

In October 2002 al-Qaida leader Ayman Zawahiri released a tape recording stating "God willing, we will continue targeting the keys of the American economy."

In September and October, the FBI broke up the Lackawana Six cell in New York.

On October 6, 2002, al-Qaida attacked a French oil tanker off the coast of Yemen, an attack that harkened back to the killing of 17 service members on the USS Cole.

On October 8, 2002, al-Qaida gunmen shot and killed a US Marine in Kuwait.

On October 12, 2002, al-Qaida affiliate Jemaah Islamiya bombed a nightclub in Bali, Indonesia, killing more than 200 and injuring about 300.

On November 28, 2002, al-Qaida fired two anti aircraft missiles at a Boeing 757 aircraft flying from

Mombassa, Kenya to Israel; suicide bombers also attacked the Paradise Hotel in Mombassa, Kenya killing 15 and injuring 40.

On December 30, 2002, three U.S. citizens were killed in Yemen during an attack on Baptist Missionary Hospital.[50]

With these events serving as the background to Kahtani's capture and detention, the Department of Defense concluded that arduous interrogation was not only a wise course of action but a proper and necessary one, as well: "The United States was clearly a country on high alert during this period and Kahtani—a known al-Qaida [sic] terrorist—was being held at Guantanamo and was believed to possess information essential to preventing future terrorist attacks."[51]

That was a sentiment echoed by John Yoo, a deputy assistant attorney general in the Office of Legal Counsel of the Department of Justice between 2001 and 2003. His job was to provide legal advice to the Bush Administration as it pertained to the fight against al-Qaeda. Raised in Philadelphia, it was Yoo who created a firestorm of public debate when he concluded that the Geneva Convention did not apply to the detainees at Gitmo.

"You never hear why they were interrogating them in the first place," Yoo said, before delving into a discussion about Kahtani specifically. "Think about it: this was a guy who, I think we have good reason to suspect, would have known where the other operatives who also might have been sent before 9/11 to the United States were, because he was one of the guys trying to get in. And so, that is exactly the kind of person that our intelligence officers should be interrogating to get information, because that guy would have a lot of information about what was going on inside the United States." He added, "I think it's a very reasonable thing to try to get that information from him—just as I think it's a very reasonable thing to try to get information from Abu Zubaydah or Khalid Sheikh Mohammed. You know, there's a reason why the country hasn't suffered another attack since September 11th—it's not just luck! I think that a lot of this good intelligence work has produced information to stop these kinds of attacks."[52]

As for the efficacy of the harsh interrogation techniques, Yoo reasoned, "It got very important information from him and from Abu Zubaydah, Khalid Sheikh Mohammed, [and] Ramzi bin al-Shibh. If you read the 9/11 Commission Report . . . how do they know all the stuff in the 9/11 Commission Report? It was only because people like Kahtani and these types of figures produced it under these kinds of interrogation methods . . . How else would we have such detailed information on how the 9/11 attacks were planned and came about and were executed? It's only because of these kinds of methods." According to Yoo, Americans may not like to hear about distasteful topics like interrogation and torture, but "that's the kind of war this is."[53]

On the other side of the debate, however, organizations like the ACLU and Amnesty International cited the fact that Kahtani was being monitored by medical professionals as an indication of potential wrongdoing and mistreatment—no matter what "kind of war" the U.S. was fighting. Consider this passage from a follow-up report in *Time Magazine* written by Adam Zagorin:

Interrogations at Guantanamo have often included a Behavioral Science Consultation Team, known as a BSCT,

on which a psychologist, psychiatrist, or other medical pro-
fessionals monitor a prisoner's ability to withstand rigor-
ous questioning. They may also suggest methods to make
the interrogation more effective. The Red Cross and the
American Medical Association have both objected to the
use of doctors to aid interrogations as a violation of medi-
cal ethics, a charge the Pentagon rejects. As [Kahtani's
attorney] put it: 'Al-Qahtani is afraid of doctors because
these are the people who would revive him and send him
back into the same interrogations that led to his pain and
physical collapse in the first place.'"[54]

Indeed, a Red Cross report compiled in 2007 and made public in April of 2009 acknowledged that medical personnel who helped facilitate interrogation techniques that had subsequently been deemed torturous were in violation of medical ethics standards. In other words, physicians or medical assistants present while a detainee was waterboarded, for instance, were found by the Red Cross to be in violation of medical ethics standards—even if they were there to ensure that the detainee didn't drown or die.[55] And on that point, the report concluded: "In the case of the alleged participation of health personnel in the detention and interrogation of the fourteen detainees, their primary purpose appears to have been to serve the interrogation process, and not the patient. In so doing the health personnel have condoned, and participated in ill-treatment."[56]

Time described the first meeting between Kahtani and his newly appointed lawyer, Gitanjali S. Gutierrez of the Center for Constitutional Rights (a New York-based nonprofit legal defense organization). Gutierrez, the report noted, wore a hejab—"a headcovering designed to shield [Kahtani] from a face-to-face encounter with his female lawyer out of respect for his sensitivities as a religious Muslim." The report continued: "A slight man in his mid 30s with short black hair and a beard, he was initially preoccupied with learning how his aging father in Saudi Arabia had contacted the lawyer, and how he could be sure that she was not another interrogator simply seeking to extract more information, Gutierrez said. 'He asked me the same questions over and over,' she added. 'His mind wandered. He engaged in long rambling monologues. He desperately sought some means of reassuring himself that I was a real lawyer and would not betray him.'"[57] A federal court ruling prohibited U.S. interrogators from listening in on those conversations. But an unclassified twenty-eight-page docket relating to Kahtani's detention throughout 2005 and 2006 now provides glimpses into the nature of the U.S. handling of Kahtani's case after his intensified interrogation ended.

The first of those twenty-eight pages briefly lays out the case as to why he was deemed an enemy combatant (defined as "an individual who was part of or supporting the Taliban or al-Qaida forces, or associated forces that are engaged in hostilities against the United States or its coalition partners. This includes any person who committed a belligerent act or has directly supported hostilities in aid of enemy armed forces.").[58] Kahtani, the October 21, 2004, document alleges, had sworn loyalty to Osama bin Laden and underwent weapons training at a camp in Afghanistan. After he was sent to the United States to "serve [his] religion" (and denied entry in Orlando on August 4, 2001), Kahtani returned to Afghanistan, eventually joined bin Laden at Tora Bora, and was subsequently apprehended in Pakistan by the Pakistani government.[59]

What follows are detailed descriptions of two Department of Defense evidence summaries compiled for the Administrative Review Board, dated October 31, 2005, and October 5, 2006. The documents, which are mostly identical aside from slight changes to the order of the information presented, exist for the stated purpose of determining if Kahtani's "continued detention is necessary."[60] Factors supporting both detention and release or transfer were presented in these summaries. In the case of both reviews, the factors offered in support of detention were far greater in number than those for release.

The detainee's level of commitment, history of training and network of connections were offered in support of his continued detention throughout 2005 and 2006. According to the documents, after he arrived in Afghanistan in early 2001, Kahtani completed several months of both basic and advanced training at the al Farouq camp, which consisted of everything from indoctrination and small weapons training to "small unit tactics and specialized weapons training." He also attended another camp, which provided tactical training, for approximately six weeks in Kandahar, Afghanistan.[61]

Kandahar is also where Kahtani swore allegiance to Osama bin Laden (in a private meeting at bin Laden's home, where Kahtani "honor[ed] and prais[ed]" the al-Qaeda leader).[62] He had also committed to completing a martyrdom mission, even though he did not know its details. His obligation to that mission, he stated, stemmed from three "fatwahs," or binding beliefs under Islamic law: to participate in jihad in Afghanistan; to swear loyalty to bin Laden; and because of that oath, to complete whatever tasks the al-Qaeda founder asked of him.[63]

Among his associations, the dockets allege, were two senior al-Qaeda members that Kahtani identified, knew, and acknowledged meeting in a safe house before 9/11. By the time of his capture in December 2001, the alleged twentieth hijacker had met personally with bin Laden four times.[64]

Most chilling of the items covered in the Administrative Review Board summaries and hearings: During an April 24, 2001, meeting, Kahtani apparently told bin Laden he'd serve the al-Qaeda leader "as he would the prophet Mohammed." Then there's this: "When asked whether he would have completed whatever mission he was assigned when going to the United States, the detainee nodded head indicating he would."[65] Two of the would-be twentieth hijacker's four meetings with bin Laden came during the summer of 2001—one before he tried to enter the United States and one afterwards.

Just two factors in favor of release or transfer were enumerated. The first, that Kahtani denied knowing anything about the September 11 attacks before they were orchestrated. Secondly, the detainee described himself as a "different person" than he'd been during the summer of 2001, and denied that he would have carried out a mission that brought about the murder of women and children.[66] Indeed, according to a transcript from his Administrative Review Board hearing, Kahtani would later say: "I understood that I would talk about who I am going to be in the future and not speak about my past."[67]

That transcript is the next item in the unclassified docket. A designated military officer and assistant presented the information contained in the Administrative Review Board briefing documents described above (according to the transcript, they read it almost verbatim) to the presiding officer and board. A board reporter and translator were present, but Kahtani's lawyer was not. The presiding military officer raised several questions, and members of the board intermittently asked questions throughout the proceeding as well. At the end of the hearing, the detainee read a written statement.

(It's important to note the following: After the designated military officer presented the relevant unclassified information to the Administrative Review Board, the transcript shows that he "requested a closed session to present classified information relevant to the disposition of the detainee." The presiding officer, the transcript notes, "acknowledged the request" before inviting Kahtani to present his statement.)[68]

Before Kahtani read the nine-page handwritten statement he had prepared for the proceeding, the assisting military officer recited a brief statement on the detainee's behalf with regards to two specific points covered in the Administrative Review Board summaries. "In response to any of the statements in the Unclassified Summary of Evidence that mention he swore *bayat* [an oath of allegiance] to Usama bin Laden or that he wanted to be a martyr, the detainee disagreed stating they were not true. The detainee stated that he told those things to the interrogators when he was being tortured a few months after he arrived at Camp X-ray, Guantanamo Bay, Cuba."[69] When the presiding officer asked Kahtani directly to confirm that statement in order to make it "very clear for the record," the detainee replied: "That is false. I have never said that [he swore *bayat* to bin Laden or wanted to be a martyr] at all."

At that point, a board member interrupted the proceeding and asked Kahtani to clarify his point further. Did he tell interrogators about his oath to bin Laden and desire to be a martyr because he was being tortured, or did he never say it at all? "Whether under torture or on my own, I have never said that I swore *bayat* to Usama bin Laden or that I wanted to be a martyr," Kahtani replied. When a board member asked directly if Kahtani had ever met with bin Laden, the detainee requested the chance to offer his testimonial, but also answered that he had not.[70]

The detainee then read aloud his statement, which he described as the first he was "making of my own will and without coercion or under the threat of torture."[71] Kahtani asserted that, contrary to his designation as an enemy combatant, he was not a threat to the United States or its allies, he had never been a threat, nor would he become one in the future. He had no knowledge of "acts of hostility" against the U.S. and wasn't a part of organizations who carried out such acts—especially against innocents, Americans or otherwise.[72]

He reported that he harbored no animosity towards the United States, despite the "torture," "cruel, inhuman, and degrading treatment," and "outrages upon my personal dignity" he had endured at Guantanamo Bay.[73] Among those offenses Kahtani listed:

Severe sleep deprivation

Severe isolation

Threat of rendition

Religious and sexual humiliation

Threats against his family

Strip and body searches and forced nudity

Denial of right to practice religion

Threats to desecrate the Koran

Stress positions

Threats by dogs

Beatings

Exposure to low temperatures

Exposure to loud music

Forcible IV pricks[74]

The combination of these, Kahtani reported to those at the proceeding, resulted in the loss of sixty pounds and required two visits to the hospital because he "was close to death during interrogation."[75] The experience at Guantanamo robbed the suspected hijacker of the "four main things in life" that a human being needs: the freedom to practice religion; personal dignity; honor (the absence of sexual humiliation); and human rights, which Kahtani believed to mean sleep, comfort, warm shelter, security, food and water, cleanliness, humane medical treatment, and the knowledge that one's family is safe. "Again, all of these rights were taken from me," he said.[76]

The stress of the physical, emotional, and psychological abuse forced Kahtani to adopt the story that he believed interrogators wanted to hear. "Interrogators provided me with this information and details and under pressure and coercion forced me to adopt the story that interrogators wanted to hear," he said.[77] The information that he provided, he reasoned, wasn't valuable and wouldn't help protect Americans or further U.S. security interests.

According to Kahtani's explanation, after the torture stopped he could not convince his captors he'd offered them falsities. He never had that opportunity. In truth, he told the Administrative Review Board, he was "a peaceful man" with no connection to terrorism, violence, or fighters, and he hadn't been allowed to defend himself by calling witnesses or compiling documents for corroboration. Nor was he allowed to consult with his lawyer.

Nevertheless, Kahtani told those present that he refused to resort to anger or revenge. In the past, he said, he enjoyed positive relationships with Americans, "and even now, I still look at Americans as human beings."[78] Indeed, Kahtani concluded, all he really wanted was to return home to Saudi Arabia. He could not answer the presiding judge's or board's questions, he told them, but his lawyer would be able to do so. "I swear to God that I did not know anything about what happened to the United States in the past. On September 11 or any other operation that happened in the past; anything that happened to you or anything that will happen to you in the future."[79]

At the conclusion of Kahtani's statement, he told the board that he would prefer to not answer their questions at that time: "The main reason is not that I am hiding anything from you, but I do not know the law." That, he said a moment later, was the order of his lawyer. The session ended without Kahtani answering questions from the board.[80]

After that encounter, Kahtani continued to maintain his assertion that he did not have any "prior knowledge of the attacks in the United States prior to their execution on 11 September 2001," according to another Administrative Review Board evidence summary dated January 17, 2008.[81] Though it adheres to the same format of the previous evidence summaries, this latest unclassified document includes several additional details. By January 2008, the Department of Defense agency responsible for reviewing Guantanamo detainees' status stated that Kahtani had confessed that he and an acquaintance had traveled to Afghanistan—with the help of "an individual who was known to facilitate the travel of prospective jihadists"—together with the intention of training for a future jihad.[82]

After Kahtani swore loyalty to bin Laden, as previous evidence summaries had established, the al-Qaeda leader deemed the young Saudi one of eight operatives fit to train specifically for the attacks planned for September 11, 2001. After his "basic country training" at al Farouq and the city training in Kandahar (according to the evidence summary, he also confirmed a list of more than twenty al-Qaeda figures he associated with while in Kandahar), Kahtani said he spent two months engaging in "firing automatic rifles and pistols while walking, running, and from moving vehicles," as well as "room clearing, kicking down doors, and jumping through windows."[83] He met five times in person with an unidentified senior al-Qaeda member, who also arranged for Kahtani to undergo Internet and e-mail training as well.

Once selected "by Usama bin Laden or another senior al Qaida leader" to participate in the plot, Kahtani received "money and travel assistance"—five or six thousand dollars and plane tickets—from a senior al-Qaeda facilitator.[84] After he was denied access at Orlando International Airport, Kahtani stated that he returned to Afghanistan and met with bin Laden on August 27, 2001. "The detainee also confirmed that he would have completed whatever mission he was assigned in the United States."[85]

That statement differed from those that favored Kahtani's release and transfer. In those statements he denied prior knowledge of the September 11 attacks and believed himself to be "a different person" than he had been in 2001. He also "thank[ed] God that he did not participate" in those attacks. "The detainee stated that his latest interviewers had coerced him into admitting that he had traveled to the United States to die. The detainee alleged that in return for this admission, these interviewers promised the detainee his freedom."[86]

What's clear from the piecing together of these various documents and news reports is that two competing perceptions are at the heart of the debate that has surrounded Mohamed al-Kahtani's interrogation for more than four years. Is he a highly trained al-Qaeda operative seeking any diversion necessary to prolong his stifled detention and eventual prosecution? Or a low-level mercenary tortured by his interrogators out of frustration or pure malice? Even the June 2005 *Time* article seemed to turn on those questions. Where Kahtani's so-called "handlers" saw traces of guilt in Kahtani's cover stories about used cars and falconry, reporters Zagorin and Duffy found other layers to the story: "In other ways, al-Kahtani emerges as an innocent abroad—uneducated, almost from another era. He asks whether the sun revolves around the earth. He wonders about dinosaurs and is told of their history and demise. He confides that he would like to marry someday—apparently not realizing how unlikely that goal now is."[87]

So how to cut to the heart of those issues? For starters, consider the written statement (taken as the equivalent of testimony) offered by 9/11 mastermind Khalid Sheikh Mohammed during the trial of Zacarias Moussaoui. Sheikh

Mohammed identified Kahtani as an operative "who came into the operation very late," and explained that, whatever his qualifications as a "muscle man" he was, nonetheless, "an extremely simple man." According to KSM, Kahtani came to him after being "presented" by Osama bin Laden himself.[88]

With bin Laden's blessing, KSM then instructed Kahtani to travel to Dubai, where he was to meet Mustafa al-Hawsawi, the al-Qaeda financier and travel agent (and the man who received a telephone call from a pay phone at Orlando International Airport on August 4, 2001). "Al-Hawsawi was to make specific arrangements for sending Al-Kahtani to the U.S. in coordination with the hijackers already in place." KSM also noted that Kahtani "was sent alone to round out the number of hijackers for the 9/11 attacks." At that point, KSM continued, Kahtani "did not know the specifics of the operation, but did understand it to be a suicide operation."[89]

After his confrontation with Melendez-Perez in Orlando on August 4, 2001, Kahtani eventually made his way back to Kandahar, Pakistan, where he again faced Sheikh Mohammed, who had little patience for his recent failure—and even less willingness to use him again. According to KSM's statement, "Al-Kahtani was selected by Bin Laden or Abu Hafs Al-Masri for the 9/11 operation, but he possessed no operational or basic knowledge that would qualify him for such an operation."[90] Kahtani, KSM noted, was unfamiliar with the process of obtaining a visa and struggled to implement the terrorist organization's system of coded communication.

An embittered Sheikh Mohammed also reflected on Kahtanti's encounter with Melendez-Perez, saying that the wannabe hijacker "made it as far as the U.S., only to be turned around at the airport and deported because he seemed too suspicious . . . al-Kahtani was too much of an unsophisticated 'bedouin' to function with ease in a modern, Western society." KSM, the statement continued, "blamed al-Kahtani's failure on facilitator al-Hawsawi because al-Hawsawi gave al-Kahtani only a one-way ticket and provided him with only limited information about his points of contacts in the U.S."[91] That, in Sheikh Mohammed's view, was the real impetus behind Kahtani's deportation.

That said, KSM clearly felt that with enough time, training, and luck even a "bedouin" like Kahtani could successfully enter the United States. The would-be twentieth hijacker "was a late addition to the operation, and, therefore, Al-Kahtani was not trained very well in dealing with customs officials or the English language." He noted that al-Qaeda's success in planting nineteen other terrorists in the United States was evidence that the September 11 planners had overestimated U.S. security measures, " . . . and as such, they did not feel they needed to train Kahtani as much. The al-Qaeda mastermind added that Kahtani was going to arrive during tourist season, a fact KSM suspected would also facilitate Kahtani's entry into the U.S.[92]

So as Kahtani claimed to be an innocent man who posed no threat to the United States, the self-proclaimed September 11 mastermind reported that bin Laden himself approved Kahtani for a mission known by the prospective hijacker to be a suicide mission. So how to navigate this apparent contradiction? Consider that Kahtani's diversions from the moment he arrived at Guantanamo through his Administrative Review Board hearing appears to correspond with large swaths of the "Manchester Document," an al-Qaeda training manual discovered by the Manchester Metropolitan Police in England during a raid of an al-Qaeda safe house.[93] Translated into English, the Manchester Document was introduced in the 2001 trial of the four terrorists who bombed U.S. embassies in Tanzania and Kenya in 1998.[94] Take note of the steps prescribed in the Manchester Document once a "brother" is summoned to a prosecution office for interrogation or questioning:

> He should, prior to questioning and whether or not he has injuries, ask the prosecutor or his representative to be seen by the medical examiner.
>
> He should, when the questioning begins, ask that evidence of his torture be entered in the report proceedings.
>
> He should, prior to the start of the questioning, ask that an attorney be present with him during the questioning process. He should mention the attorney by name.
>
> He should ask for food.
>
> He should deny all information [accusations] about him by the prosecution representative. He should claim that the interrogation apparatus has fabricated those accusations and should deny his connection to anything obtained against him.
>
> The brother may have to confess under pressure of torture in the interrogation center. Once in the prosecution center, however, he should say that he was tortured, deny all his prior confessions, and ask that the interrogation be repeated.[95]

In fact, the document's eighteenth and final chapter is dedicated to providing instruction in case a "brother" finds himself in a prison or detention center. The first nugget of advice offered is this: "At the beginning of the trial, once more the brothers must insist on proving that torture was inflicted on them by State Security [investigators] before the judge." The next entry? "Complain [to the court] of mistreatment while in prison." A hunger strike, meanwhile, is deemed "possible" but also "a tactic that can either succeed or fail."[96]

Kahtani's training—minimal as it was, perhaps—seems nevertheless to have proven successful. Fast forward to May of 2008. Susan Crawford, who as convening authority of military commissions was in charge of determining whether to bring Guantanamo Bay detainees to trial, announced that war crimes charges against Kahtani would be dismissed.[97] At the time, no reason for the dismissal was offered, and in the fall of 2008, military prosecutors announced plans to refile charges against Kahtani based on evidence independent of that which the detainee offered during his interrogation.[98]

But in January of 2009, Crawford told the *Washington Post* that she had reviewed the interrogation techniques Kahtani had been subjected to at Guantanamo between November of 2002 and January of 2003 and now believed they had "met the legal definition of torture."[99] Kahtani's lawyers said they believed those harsh techniques made it unlikely that their client could be prosecuted. The treatment, they said, "left him a broken man who has attempted suicide," according to the *New York Times*.[100]

When Crawford announced the reason for the dismissal, the Pentagon issued a statement that referenced "more than a dozen investigations and reviews of our detention operations" en route to concluding that those methods—including those used specifically on Kahtani—were legal. Since Kahtani's interrogation, the department noted, the Pentagon had adopted stricter guidelines for such encounters.[101] In other words, some of the techniques used on the supposed twentieth hijacker had been restricted after the fact. Crawford explained: "The techniques they used were all authorized, but the manner in which they applied them was overly aggressive and too persistent . . . You think of torture, you think of some horrendous physical act done to an individual. This was not any one particular act; this was just a combination of things that had a medical impact on him, that hurt his health. It was abusive and uncalled for. And coercive. Clearly coercive."[102]

Meanwhile, the *Washington Post* reported, Crawford allowed charges against five other 9/11 detainees—including Khalid Sheikh Mohammed, who unlike Kahtani, is known to have been waterboarded—to go forward because investigators proved to her that they'd built a viable case outside of information gathered during the interrogations. Kahtani's prosecutors, she told the *Post*'s Bob Woodward, were "unprepared." "A prosecutor has an ethical obligation to review all the evidence before making a charging decision. And they didn't have access to all the evidence, including medical records, interrogation logs, and they were making charging decisions without looking at everything."[103]

As it would turn out, the world would get a closer look at the "everything" Crawford referred to when, in April of 2009, the Justice Department released four of the infamous "torture memos," written by attorneys in the department's Office of Legal Counsel in August of 2002 and May of 2005. Not only did those memos reveal the legal impetus behind the Bush administration's decision to approve coercive interrogation methods in limited doses for high-value al-Qaeda operatives, they also laid out in full detail the nature of those interrogation methods. Among them: Forced nudity, sleep deprivation, walling (slamming a detainee into a flexible wall constructed to create a loud sound upon impact) and cramped confinement. Also given the blow-by-blow treatment was the process of waterboarding, which Attorney General Eric Holder deemed illegal.[104]

President Obama made a point of publicly assuring that the CIA agents who physically implemented and oversaw the enhanced interrogations would not be prosecuted for carrying out their jobs as legally prescribed at the time. He also reiterated his unwillingness to embark upon an investigation into the programs and his predecessor's legal arguments justifying them.[105]

Nevertheless, the release of the memos represented the Obama administration's closing of what the President called a "dark and painful chapter in our history."[106] Nearly three months after he announced his intention to shutter the prison at the naval base at Guantanamo Bay, he pledged that the U.S. would never employ the techniques again.[107]

Newspaper editorials throughout the country praised President Obama's handling of the issue. The *New York Times* lamented: "To read the four newly released memos on prisoner interrogation written by George W. Bush's Justice Department is to take a journey into depravity."[108] "Almost as shocking as the documents' catalog of cruelties are the Orwellian arguments with which their authors rationalized waterboarding, the withholding of food and other violations of human dignity," wrote the *Los Angeles Times*.[109] Under the headline "Dealing with a Disgrace," the editorial board at the *Washington Post* had this to say: "By repudiating the memos, the Obama administration has again seized the high ground and restored some of the honor lost over the past few years. President Obama's actions not only restore confidence that this country will not torture, but he has also strengthened the nation's moral authority in condemning these heinous acts wherever they occur."[110]

Perhaps unsurprisingly, there was no shortage of vitriol towards the Bush administration and the lawyers who wrote those four legal memos. But one treatment written in defense of the memos, authored by former CIA director General Michael Hayden and former Attorney General Michael Mukasey, was especially insightful.

Writing in the *Wall Street Journal*, Hayden and Mukasey made perhaps the most succinct, tenable case in support of the efficacy of keeping torture open as an option for U.S. interrogators. Releasing the memos, they wrote, amounted not only to "unsound" policy—but also one whose "effect will be to invite the kind of institutional timidity and fear of recrimination that weakened intelligence gathering in the past, and that we came sorely to regret on Sept. 11, 2001."[111]

Hayden and Mukasey then dissembled what they deemed the four central arguments supporting the release of the memos. First, with regards to the idea that the CIA had already halted the interrogation program (and so making its details public was acceptable), they argued that the public airing of the documents now assured that terrorists could bolster their resistance training accordingly. Why? Because our enemies were made aware of the "absolute limit of what the U.S. government could do to extract information from them"—a knowledge that would "diminish the effectiveness of these techniques" as they had others in the past.[112] In other words, where the Manchester Document gave terrorists a window into potential scenarios they'd face once in the interrogation room, the Obama administration had just offered a complete tour of U.S. tactics.

Hayden and Mukasey then launched into a critique of the "ignorant" belief that the harsh interrogation program was unsuccessful and ineffective. They used the example of Abu Zubaydah—a case maligned not a month before in a *Washington Post* article headlined "Detainee's Harsh Treatment Foiled No Plots"[113]—to bolster their case. Under the CIA's coercive interrogation, Zubaydah (who, the authors note, had given up some information before the enhanced measures began) revealed information that led to the apprehension of 9/11 planner Ramzi bin al Shibh. Al Shibh subsequently provided information that amounted to the capture of Khalid Sheikh Mohammed. The authors noted: " . . . Intelligence can be verified, correlated and used to get information from other detainees, and has been," they wrote. "None of this information is used in isolation."[114]

And contrary to what was becoming conventional wisdom with each successive news report on the enhanced techniques, the methods used to obtain that information was not released by legal necessity, Hayden and Mukasey wrote. "Even when the government disclosed that three members of al-Qaeda had been subjected to waterboarding but that the technique was no longer part of the CIA interrogation program," the piece reads, "the court sustained the government's argument that the precise details of how it was done, including limits and safeguards, could remain classified against the possibility that some future president may authorize its use."[115] There was no legal reason—even in the face of a deadline imposed by an ACLU lawsuit—that the Obama administration couldn't simply rehash the argument.

Finally, Hayden and Mukasey arrived at the most pervasive argument in favor of wiping the option of torture off the table: the idea that it had darkened U.S. standing in the world. That claim, they wrote, "conflates interrogation with the sadism" of a few knuckleheads out of 140,000 at Abu Ghraib.[116] And at what cost? Hayden and Mukasey believe that it served to nullify any faith that investigators—and indeed, future presidents—could realistically reserve for memos sought and submitted by the Office of Legal Counsel. "Those charged with the responsibility of gathering potentially lifesaving information from unwilling captives are now told essentially that any legal opinion they get as to the lawfulness of their activity is only as durable as political fashion permits," they wrote.[117] The threat of after-the-fact public exposure, meanwhile, would make interrogators and their legal advisors each think twice.

The result? The completion of another cycle like the one that culminated with the attacks of September 11, 2001: Intelligence gatherers are pressured to push the legal limits; that aggressiveness loses its political viability; arguments of restraint carry the day; and finally, the intelligence community is left—as it was after 9/11, the authors note—to take criticism for its "feckless timidity" on the chin.[118]

A FIELD OF HONOR

On April 12, 2006, I received my first opportunity to introduce Jose Melendez-Perez to a national audience. By that time, my Philadelphia radio listeners had become well acquainted with Melendez-Perez's incredible story, but I felt strongly that the nation as a whole needed to hear about this little-known hero of September 11. I finally got my chance when I was asked to fill in for my good friend Joe Scarborough as guest host of his MSNBC program, *Scarborough Country*. The prevailing news story of that day was the ongoing trial of Zacarias Moussaoui, and specifically the fact that jurors were allowed to hear for themselves the actual flight recordings of the final thirty minutes of Flight 93. Until that day, the only people who had been permitted to hear those tapes were the family members of the people who died aboard the flight and federal investigators. As would be expected, the entire courtroom was transfixed by the final sounds from inside the plane just before it crashed into a field in southwestern Pennsylvania. The government's case against Moussaoui centered on the idea that if Moussaoui had his wish, he would have joined the nineteen other fanatics who attacked the World Trade Center and the Pentagon. As a guest-host with a national audience, I had the perfect opportunity to introduce the man the 9/11 Commission had explicitly credited with stopping another would-be 9/11 hijacker—the man whose actions contributed to the passenger uprising by depriving the terrorists of the added "muscle" of Mohamed al-Kahtani.

I asked Melendez-Perez whether he was still an anomaly among border security personnel. I wanted to know, in other words, whether the federal government was holding up his actions, as well as those of Diana Dean, as models for proper visitor inspection and questioning protocol. Had he seen a change in the training of border inspectors since September 11—a movement towards fostering and developing street smarts? "Well, I think that we have learned our lesson. Since we became Customs and Border Protection, we've taken care of all those nonsense policies that treated visitors from certain countries in a special way. Now only one set of rules applies to all," Melendez-Perez answered.

"And that set of rules means that anybody who we think is coming to this country to do any harm, or to add to the population of illegal immigrants, we now have the mechanism to get them out. Fortunately, CBP headquarters has provided us with all the mechanisms and all the support that we need to accomplish our mission. Also, we have a great training program, in which we are going in the right direction to ensure that what happened doesn't happen again. And we learned the lesson. And we have to be thankful for that."[1]

Due to the efforts of Jose Melendez-Perez, our nation was spared further loss of life that would have occurred had Flight 93 reached its intended target. Although the hijackers failed, Flight 93 crashed at a speed of more than 500 m.p.h. into a field in Western Pennsylvania's Somerset County near the town of Shanksville. Along with family members and loved ones, a steady stream of grateful Americans began visiting this desolate, windswept field to pay their respects. Soon after, a makeshift memorial overlooking the crash site was created to serve as a meeting place for the nearly 130,000 annual visitors who began to descend on the area.[2] Former

Governor Mark Schweiker (who assumed that office when his predecessor Tom Ridge became the first head of the Department of Homeland Security) explained the charged atmosphere of the place in the wake of the crash: "Shanksville is a word that still evokes so much emotion for me. My first moments there are still frozen in [my] mind because you can never shake the horrible images of that crash site. It was a place that sat tranquil for centuries. The trees and rolling hills were beautiful. Then all of a sudden, in the middle of it was such devastation. Like everything that happened on September 11, none of it seemed to make sense."[3]

Prior to September 11, Shanksville, Pennsylvania, was unknown to most Americans—and but for the heroic actions of the passengers and crew, the area would have remained out of the national lexicon. For the most part though, as the months and years began to elapse since the attacks, things settled back into the quiet rhythms of daily life.

Quiet, that is, until the fall of 2005, when hundreds of blogs became electrified by a controversy surrounding the proposed memorial to the passengers of Flight 93. Not long after the nation mourned the events of September 11, many felt it was important to safeguard that quiet, reclaimed strip mine where forty passengers and crew members had perished by creating a memorial to honor their heroic efforts. On September 24, 2002, President Bush signed the Flight 93 National Memorial Act into law, which secured federal funding for such a project.[4] A design competition was held and the committee charged with selecting the design—a group that included design professionals, community leaders, and family members of the victims—chose the entry entitled "The Crescent of Embrace" submitted by Paul and Milena Murdoch.[5]

At the center of the blogger protests was the fact that the title of the winning proposal contained the word "crescent." The proposal envisioned indigenous red maple trees to be planted in a semicircle opposite the crash site. Irate bloggers showcased animated color graphics that featured an Islamic symbol superimposed over the contemplated row of maple trees. Many questioned just how the memorial's planners could justify the inclusion of what appeared to be a red Islamic crescent at the very spot where radical Islam killed forty innocent people aboard Flight 93.

According to defenders of the memorial, however, the surrounding topography alone dictated the Murdochs' positioning of these maples. No association with or reference to Islam was intended. As the design bid invitation recognized, "The bowl-like topography of the area is defined by higher elevations of land to the north and west. The area includes both natural and reclaimed landscapes. The Temporary Memorial is located within this zone, as is the grassy mound used by the families to view the crash site on their initial visits . . . the Bowl provides views to and from the Sacred Ground and could be the focus of the visitor experience."[6] Therefore, it was this bowl—not some secret intention on the part of the designers—that formed the crescent shape that characterized the Murdochs' plan. In reality, a very deliberate process had been carefully planned and followed—a process that sparked great enthusiasm and interest across the country. And for all the inflamed rhetoric of the blogosphere, only one letter of official public comment raised the crescent complaint. Furthermore, there was never any kind of organized opposition from those who matter most—the families and loved ones of the victims. The design was, nevertheless, easily ridiculed from afar and without firsthand knowledge of the situation, I found the issue worthy of further examination.

At the urging of former U.S. Senator Rick Santorum and Ed Root, a retired business analyst who lost his cousin Lorraine Bay on Flight 93, I decided on a whim to go to Shanksville and take a look for myself. I announced my intentions on my radio program and soon realized that many of my listeners were eager to join me. The interest was overwhelming and we actually had to limit the number of participants, as buses were scarce due to a Penn State home football game. On a crisp September morning, forty-seven of my radio listeners joined my staff and me on a journey to find out for ourselves if the controversy was real or contrived. Having served as a juror in the selection process responsible for the final design, Root—who was along for the ride—was highly knowledgeable about the proposed memorial and not only led my tour but also coordinated with National Park Service project manager Jeff Reinbold to give us an in-depth brief of the site and future plans.

When we visited the site of the crash of Flight 93 we found the temporary memorial overlooking the actual crash site about five hundred yards away. The makeshift memorial consisted of a forty-foot section of chain-link fence—one foot for each of the forty passengers and crew who lost their lives—canvassed with cards, letters, artwork, flowers, and other memorabilia deposited by visitors just like us who had found it an essential part of the recovery process to visit this tranquil site. Some visitors to the site were simply content to sign a nearby highway guardrail. By the time of our visit in 2005, the temporary memorial was averaging more than 130,000 visitors annually from all fifty states and numerous countries around the world.[7] That day, I remember seeing cars from Texas and Colorado in the overcrowded parking lot. Even without the trappings of a traditional memorial, the site was hallowed ground. People were drawn to this unassuming corner of southwestern Pennsylvania to quietly mourn those who had lost their lives on September 11 and to honor the fight of the passengers and crew of Flight 93.

No one in the quintessential Middle American town is cashing in on their new status as a tourist attraction. I actually had trouble finding a "Let's roll!" T-shirt when we stopped at a nearby general store as we prepared for our trip home. The site is ably run by the National Park Service with the help of a group of "ambassadors"—an extraordinary group of dozens of local residents whose lives have changed in ways they could have never imagined before the attacks of September 11. These dedicated volunteers greet visitors, answer questions about the story of Flight 93, and maintain the temporary memorial ten hours a day, seven days a week, 365 days a year—a daunting yet noble task that anyone who has experienced the merciless weather at the former strip mine can appreciate.

Throughout our tour, Jeff Reinbold from the National Park Service struck me as a thoughtful and well-meaning planner. On the day of our visit, he showed up early in the morning with architectural renderings under his arm and his three-year-old son in tow, anxious to explain the permanent memorial's selection process. It was evident that he cared deeply about the memorial and the people it represented, even if he had never met a single soul from Flight 93. He also said the memorial in Shanksville represented the first time the National Park Service used a competition to design an entire national park, which, in this case, is about 1,000 acres. He described the challenge confronting the memorial's prospective designers like this: "How do you come up with a fitting tribute to the passengers of Fight 93, and do it in a way that can be successful on this landscape?" [8]

On the bus ride to and from Shanksville, we watched movie treatments about the flight—A&E's *Flight 93* and the Discovery Channel's *The Flight that Fought Back*. The next year, another movie would be released amid understandable claims that it was "too soon." In 2006, the film *United 93* became the first major motion picture to dramatize the events that unfolded in Newark and over Pennsylvania. If you've only heard or read about it, you need to watch this powerful, inspiring movie. Some were concerned about Hollywood's ability to tell the story without making a political statement, while others were convinced that *Flight 93* and *The Flight that Fought Back* had already presented an accurate and complete accounting of the flight. *United 93* writer/director Paul Greengrass—the man who directed *The Bourne Supremacy*—deserves a great deal of credit for ignoring his critics and creating an honorably accurate film. Many were poised to blow the whistle if he got it wrong or distorted either memory or facts, but instead there seemed to be universal acceptance of his final product. In arguably the most politically charged environment in our history, Greengrass was able to make a movie about a historical event in a manner devoid of politics.

United 93 is a movie incredibly well filmed and scored. The jerky nature of the footage befits the events, and the sound that accompanies the imagery is just right. The reality that comes from the scenes filmed inside the aircraft is haunting. What I found most significant was that the movie features no "stars"—rather it's an epic about American history and real Americans. Heroic Americans. Men and women of various ages and walks of life. Thirty-three passengers and seven crew members who defied four terrorists. As far as the story is told, there are no standouts among the passengers, which is a good thing too. While they bear identifying qualities that will ring true to their loved ones, their identities are not front and center, and a deliberate effort was made not to assert the personas of any of them. They are treated as equals.

Another one of my major concerns before seeing the film was its potential to be exploited by our enemies. Fortunately, there is no chance that this film will have propaganda value for radical Islam. While there is no effort to embellish what the passengers did, there is also no false treatment of the terrorists, nor exaggeration of their failure. The film is remarkably true to the facts—both good and bad alike. Indeed, issues of government ineptitude leading up to the actual attacks weren't ignored. While the movie doesn't point fingers, it documents plenty of ill-equipped government actors and an abundance of chaos.

There were reportedly cries of "too soon" when a trailer was shown at the famed Grauman's Chinese Theater in Hollywood. *Variety* reported that while many men were anxious to see *United 93*, the film also received a high percentage of "definitely not interested" feedback, which was unfortunate.[9]

In my case, I had the surreal experience of seeing it with a local woman who bears the emotional scars of what happened that day. Ellen Saracini, the widow of United Airlines Flight 175 pilot Victor Saracini, whose flight was referenced time and again by the traffic controllers in *United 93*, was there the same night as I was. "What is going through her mind right now?" I wondered. Suddenly, my popcorn seemed totally inappropriate.

One of Greengrass's most brilliant directorial touches is that the film takes place in real time. Flight 93 from Newark, New Jersey, to San Francisco, departed at 8:42 on September 11, 2001, four minutes before Flight 11 hit the North Tower. It ended up in a former strip mine in Shanksville, Pennsylvania at 10:03 a.m. (twenty minutes shy of Washington, D.C.). Accounting for preflight activities, that is about as long as you'll spend watching the events unfold onscreen. During that time, attention is paid not only to what was occurring in the fuselage, but also with the interplay between the FAA command center in Herndon, Virginia, and various control towers in Boston, New York, Cleveland, and SAG command in Rome, NewYork. While the gruesome nature of what occurred onboard is fully evident, there is no effort made to accentuate the violence of that day either on this airplane or any of the others. You won't see computer-generated animation or special effects—in fact, you'll see actual footage of the planes hitting the Twin Towers. Perhaps the most amazing aspect of the film was that even though we all know the ending, the climax is still a suspenseful moment. For the first time, Americans who heard the sounds recorded on the aircraft's cockpit voice recorder, or read the transcripts from that device, could associate what happened in those final five minutes with imagery:

09:35:40 — "I don't want to die."

09:35:41 — "No, no. Down, down."

09:35:42 — "I don't want to die. I don't want to die."

09:35:44 — "No, no. Down, down, down, down, down, down."

09:35:47 — "No, no, please."

09:35:57 — "No."

09:37:06 — "That's it. Go back."

09:37:06 — "That's it. Sit down."

09:37:36 — "Everything is fine. I finished."[10]

The jurors in the Moussaoui trial were allowed to hear these actual recordings; it was the first time they'd been played in public. At the time, Neil Lewis reported in the *New York Times*: "Although the general story of Flight 93 based on such official investigations has been known for some time, listening to the audio seemed nonetheless a harrowing experience for the jurors." I believe it should be a harrowing experience for us all—to hear the horror and recognize the heroism of the passengers of Flight 93 seconds before crashing into the field in Shanksville. The violence in the cabin convinced the passengers that this wasn't just an ordinary hijacking. Jurors in the Moussaoui case heard the phone call of Marion Britton, a passenger, to a friend on the ground. "Don't worry," the friend consoled. "They'll probably take you to another country." Ms. Britton replied, "Two passengers have had their throats cut."[11] The voice recordings captured the final words of the hijackers as well as the voices of passengers as they began to storm the cockpit:

10:00:22 — "Oh Allah, oh Allah, oh gracious."

10:00:25 — "In the cockpit. If we don't, we'll die."

10:01:08 — "Is that it? I mean, shall we pull it down?"

10:01:09 — "Yes, put it in, and pull it down."

10:03:02 — "Allah is the greatest."[12]

The actions of Jose Melendez-Perez had a direct effect on the outcome of 9/11—tipping the balance in favor of the passengers of Flight 93. In the final moments of that ill-fated flight, the passengers rallied heroically behind guys like Mark Bingham, a six-foot, four-inch, 225-pound rugby player who once ran with the bulls in Pamplona. As Karen Breslau noted in a *Newsweek* piece about those final five minutes: "Investigators are operating on the theory that the men somehow made their way up 100 feet from the rear of the plane into the cockpit. The last transmission recorded is someone, probably a hijacker, screaming 'Get out of here. Get out of here.' Then grunting, screaming and scuffling. Then silence."[13]

There is no denying the powerful and stirring character of the current temporary memorial at Shanksville. The forty-foot section of chainlinked fence has provided comfort and a place to pay respects for the countless people who have been driven to visit the site since September 11. The Ambassadors and National Park Service members are a testament to the resolve of the American people and our ability to stand triumphantly in the face of great tragedy. That being said, the passengers of Flight 93 deserve a more lasting tribute to their bravery. The need for a permanent memorial that can serve as a place of mourning and as a place to tell the story of the heroics of the day is clear. Despite the controversy that ensued after the initial design was presented to the public, this necessity has never been in doubt.

Former Pennsylvania Governor Schweiker reflected on the crucial importance of this memorial site: "It really wasn't until I attended the one-year mark of the terrorist attacks in

Shanksville that I realized this episode was far from over. A site that had made so many Americans feel sorry and despair became inspiring that day. It was a day that not only allowed us to move past those terrible events, but it allowed all of us to reflect on the incredible heroism that was displayed on Flight 93. It was clear to everyone that those brave souls began the fight back against terrorism in the skies above Pennsylvania 9/11. That fact is indisputable. They didn't have weapons; they weren't trained military personnel; they were ordinary Americans who did an extraordinary thing. They knew they were going to die, but they were still determined to save others. They were our modern day Minutemen."[14]

And since so many people from such great distances have felt called to this sparse, lonely landscape—over one million as of this writing[15]—several groups of generous, patriotic Americans have teamed together to build a permanent national memorial to the passengers of Flight 93. These groups include the Families of Flight 93, Inc., a 501(C) 3 organization wishing to hallow the sacred ground of their fallen loved ones in a fitting way; the fifteen-member Flight 93 Federal Advisory Commission, which comprises family members, local residents, and the director of the National Park Service; and the Commission's operational arm, the Flight 93 Memorial Task Force, composed of nearly one hundred people from a wide variety of vocations who all share an interest and concern in planning and designing the memorial. The permanent site will be a living monument and learning center teaching all future generations about the events of September 11. It will strive to draw meaning and significance from the actions of the passengers and crew on that fateful day when they became the first casualties of the war on terror.

The Mission Statement of the Flight 93 National Memorial calls for a memorial that

Honors the passengers and crew of Flight 93 who courageously gave their lives, thereby thwarting a planned attack on Washington, D.C.

Allows the public to visit the site and express feelings about the event and the passengers and crew of Flight 93.

Respects the rural landscape and preserves the solemn and tranquil setting of the crash site of Flight 93.[16]

To accomplish these goals, the partners engaged in the memorial project have long been at work putting into action a carefully thought-out plan. As the Flight 93 National Memorial Project's official Mission Statement states regarding the design process alone: "We have followed a careful, open and inclusive yearlong design process in arriving at this point. This process allowed for public comments and review of the submitted designs both in person and online. This process included two juries, Stage I and Stage II, whose responsibility it was to select a final design. Each jury included family members as well as design and art professionals and business leaders."[17]

While the Flight 93 National Memorial Act signed by President Bush in 2002 secured funding for the project, it alone is not enough to complete all phases of the proposed memorial. Between land acquisition and construction costs, it is estimated that it would take almost $58 million to compete the project. The federal government and the government of the Commonwealth of Pennsylvania pledged to provide nearly $28 million. The rest would be raised from private funds by the Flight 93 National Memorial Campaign.[18] Because the memorial is to be completed in phases, not all of the private funding is needed at once. The first phase—which includes the circular memorial of maple trees and visitor center—is scheduled to begin construction by the end of 2009 and is expected to be completed in time for the tenth anniversary of 9/11. As of this writing, all but $3 million has been raised for the first phase and planners are confident that the project is on schedule for the September 11, 2011, dedication.[19] In June of 2011, the federal government—in pursuit of the final 500 acres needed for the memorial—issued an ultimatum to the private citizens who owned that land.[20]

The individuals committed to maintaining the temporary memorial as its permanent incarnation is developed are thoughtful, dedicated people who want to welcome and encourage public participation at each stage of the planning and construction of this new national memorial. Knowing these committed professionals and volunteers, I now understand the plan far better than the images on my computer led me to believe. I no longer object to the design—nor do the listeners who took the time to travel to Shanksville with me. In fact, I have pledged to do all that I can to support fundraising efforts for the memorial's construction. Since our visit to the crash site in 2005, the project designers have revisited the issue to alleviate the American public's concerns. Nobody wanted any sort of controversy to stigmatize this hallowed ground. The Murdochs' solution was to complete the crescent—transforming it into a circle embracing the final resting place of these 9/11 heroes. The entrance to the circle follows the flight path of the plane. The word "crescent" was dropped.

Beyond its careful handling of the crescent controversy, the project partnership is very sensitive to how private and federal dollars are spent. For example, rather than compelling the government to buy an exorbitant amount of the local land surrounding the crash site, planners are working to purchase only enough surrounding parkland to ensure the serenity and dignity of the national memorial while remaining conscious of convenient access for future visitors as well as the properties of local residents. As of this writing, most of the land needed for the memorial has been acquired. The permanent memorial will also house, under the custodianship of the National Park Service, the collection of more than 20,000 tributes left at the temporary memorial since September 11, 2001. "So many have journeyed so far to this remote place inspired by the actions of the heroes of Flight 93. It is the purity of this pilgrimage that testifies so eloquently to the strength of these peaceful fields. The full emotional and educational journey will be completed with the dedication of the permanent Flight 93 National Memorial on September 11, 2011," said Joanne Hanley, a National Park Service superintendent at the Flight 93 National Memorial.[21]

Quite fittingly, this partnership to build a permanent national memorial to the heroes of Flight 93 has taken this motto: "A common field one day. A field of honor forever."

They are the words of a Los Angeles city fireman, Captain Stephen Ruda. I can't improve upon them. They inspire us to "remember the collective acts of courage and sacrifice of the passengers and crew, revere this hallowed ground as the final resting place of those heroes, and reflect on the power of individuals who choose to make a difference."[22] I hope that they will also inspire you to support these fellow Americans in this most worthy endeavor.

By purchasing this book, you have assisted with the construction of the permanent memorial. To do more visit www .honorflight93.org or mail your donation to:

Flight 93 National Memorial Campaign
c/o National Park Foundation
1201 Eye St, NW, Suite 550B
Washington, DC 20005

Thank you,
Michael A. Smerconish
September 8, 2009

ACKNOWLEDGMENTS

William Anthony: As the acting assistant commissioner of the Office of Public Affairs, U.S. Customs and Border Protection, Department of Homeland Security, Bill has been wholeheartedly supportive of my efforts to tell Jose's story. Throughout the research and writing of this book, he was an invaluable source of guidance, information, and insight on CBP policies and personnel. Many of the interviews conducted in these pages were made possible thanks to Bill, and I'm deeply appreciative of his assistance.

Josh Belfer: Josh Belfer is a former intern and current student at the University of Pennsylvania who provided his usual stellar research and fact-checking for this project, and submitted a comprehensive gut check in its final weeks.

Donna Glessner: A volunteer at the Flight 93 National Memorial, Donna Glessner's meticulous fact-checking and review of portions of this book were crucial to making it a true a representation of the actions of the forty heroes aboard Flight 93.

Ben Haney: Another former intern, Notre Dame student Ben Haney—fresh off a stint working for the McCain-Palin campaign—provided timely fact-checking and research as this book came together.

John McDonald: As has become his custom, John McDonald became involved in this project midstream. At a time when there was no light at the end of the tunnel, his perseverance and competency gave it direction and put it on a path toward completion. Truly, John is deserving of tremendous credit for seeing this project to completion. His responsibilities required that he become well versed in complex facts within a very short period of time, integrate ever-changing publicly available information, and synthesize competing drafts. But for his work, Jose's story would not have been told in timely fashion. He is a quiet force of strength for all of my written and spoken projects and a valued member of my team.

William McSwain, Esq.: A former marine and assistant U.S. Attorney, Bill McSwain was the executive director of the Church Report, released in 2005. He has firsthand experience with the most controversial interrogation techniques detailed here and became a willing and knowledgeable resource as this book progressed.

Hamilton Peterson, Esq.: Hamilton Peterson understands better than most the importance of protecting America in the wake of the attacks perpetrated on September 11, 2001. The president of the Board of Families of Flight 93, Hamilton lost his father Donald and stepmother Jean on September 11. I'm honored that his expertise is a part of this book.

Jeff Reinbold: The National Park Service project manager for the Flight 93 National Memorial, Jeff Reinbold has on more than one occasion taken the time to explain to my radio listeners and me the deliberations that went into the design of the Flight 93 National Memorial. He was a courteous, competent and wonderful tour guide.

Ed Root: Ed Root is a retired business analyst who lost his cousin, Lorraine Bay, on Flight 93. He served as a juror in the selection process for the final design of the Flight 93 National Memorial and has been a reliable liaison between the authors and those involved in the planning of the memorial, including members of the National Park Service. Thank you, Ed. You fueled my desire to tell an important back story to a flight on which you lost a loved one.

Mary Russel: As in the days of my private practice as an attorney with the Beasley Law Firm in Philadelphia, Mary has gone above and beyond the call in her secretarial duties. Her attention to detail, commitment, and tireless work ethic are at a level of perfection that I like to call "old school." They don't make 'em like Mary anymore, and she made sure that this book was worthy of the subject matter it contains.

Edward Ryan: Many thanks to this acting United States Attorney who is prosecuting the 9/11 conspirators, including Kahtani. Within the limitations of his professional role, Mr. Ryan was nevertheless invaluable as a resource concerning publicly available documents relevant in this story.

Thank you to everyone at Lyons Press—including Scott Watrous, Gene Brissie, Inger Forland—for recognizing the heroism Jose Melendez-Perez displayed in August of 2001 and allowing me to tell his story. Thank you Marina Ein for so ably serving as literary publicist. Thanks as well to my literary agent, Larry Kirshbaum, and to George Hiltzik, who represents me in all my radio and television endeavors.

Both of my nationally syndicated radio shows thrive because of the dedication and intelligence of executive producer T.C. Scornavacchi and the expertise of technical producer Greg Stocker. Also among the interns who I refuse to let cut the cord, special thanks goes to Anthony Mazzarelli, who I'm sure would hit Google right now if I asked him for a bit of research—regardless of M.D. and Esq. tags that now follow his name.

The six hours of radio content we produce is reaching new cities and engaging new listeners every day thanks to my partnership with the good people at Dial Global, including David Landau, Spencer Brown, Amy Bolton, John Murphy, Jessica Sherman and Donna Harrison. Thirty-five hours a week of listening, every week, is all we ask!

Back at home base in Philadelphia, I'm indebted to everyone at The Big Talker 1210, including Marc Rayfield, David Yadgaroff, Andy Bloom, Ed Palladino, Mike Baldini and Cindy Webster. Many thanks to Walter Kosc for so ably managing our promotional campaigns and events; to Frank Canale, Dave Skalish, "Dr." Bart Feroe and Tommy MacDonald for your technical prowess; and to Rob Kaloustian and the sales team converting my radio content into cash.

I'm thankful as well to Steve Capus, Phil Griffin, and Chris Matthews for my relationship with MSNBC.

ENDNOTES

Introduction

1. National Commission on Terrorist Attacks upon the United States, Public Hearing, January 26, 2004, www .globalsecurity.org/security/library/congress/9-11_ commission/040126-transcript.htm.

2. Ibid.

3. John Lehman, "Our Enemy is not Terrorism," *Proceedings*, March 31, 2004, www.johnflehman.com/pdf/ proceedings_MAR2004.pdf.

4. National Commission on Terrorist Attacks upon the United States.

Chapter One

1. Various government agencies and news reports provide differing spellings of Mohamed al-Kahtani's name.

2. Statement of Jose E. Melendez-Perez to the National Commission on Terrorist Attacks upon the United States, Seventh Public Hearing, January 26, 2004, www.9-11commission .gov/hearings/hearing7/witness_melendez.htm.

3. Ellen Nakashima and Spencer Hsu, "U.S. plans to screen all who enter, leave country," *Washington Post*, November 3, 2006, www.washingtonpost.com/wp-dyn/ content/article/2006/11/02/AR2006110201810_pf.html.

4. Statement of Jose E. Melendez-Perez to the National Commission on Terrorist Attacks Upon the United States.

5. Between 2006 and 2009, the author conducted a series of interviews with Jose Melendez-Perez. This manuscript includes many direct quotes, facts, and reflections from

those interviews. This series will henceforth be cited as follows: Jose Melendez-Perez, interview by Michael Smerconish.

6. Ibid.

7. Ibid.

8. Ibid.

Chapter Two

1. Jose Melendez-Perez, interview by Michael Smerconish.

2. Ibid.

3. "Fort Buchanan History," U.S. Army Installation Management Command, Southeast Region,www.buchanan .army.mil/sites/about/history.asp.

4. Jose Melendez-Perez, interview by Michael Smerconish.

5. Ibid.

6. Ibid.

7. George Johnson, "Portrait of the 1980s: Back in 1979, the word was malaise," *New York Times*, December 24, 1989, www.nytimes.com/1989/12/24/weekinreview/portrait-of-the-1980-s-back-in-1979-the-word-was-malaise.html.

8. "Glynco," Federal Law Enforcement Training Center, U.S. Department of Homeland Security, www.fletc.gov/ about-fletc/locations/glynco.

9. Jose Melendez-Perez, interview by Michael Smerconish.

10. Ibid.

11. Statement of Robert C. Bonner to the National Commission on Terrorist Attacks Upon the United States, Seventh Public Hearing, January 26, 2004, www.9-11commission.gov/ hearings/hearing7/witness_bonner.htm.

12. Jose Melendez-Perez, interview by Michael Smerconish.

13. Ibid.

14. Ibid.

15. Ibid.

16. Ibid.

Chapter Three

1. Statement of Jose E. Melendez-Perez to the National Commission on Terrorist Attacks Upon the United States, Seventh Public Hearing, January 26, 2004, www.9-11commission .gov/hearings/hearing7/witness_melendez.htm.

2. Jose Melendez-Perez, interview by Michael Smerconish.

3. Ibid.

4. Statement of Jose E. Melendez-Perez to the National Commission on Terrorist Attacks Upon the United States.

5. Jose Melendez-Perez, interview by Michael Smerconish.

6. Statement of Jose E. Melendez-Perez to the National Commission on Terrorist Attacks Upon the United States.

7. Jose Melendez-Perez, interview by Michael Smerconish.

8. Ibid.

9. "Terrorism 101: A How-To Guide" [The Manchester Document], The Smoking Gun, www.thesmokinggun.com/ archive/jihadmanual.html.

10. Statement of Jose E. Melendez-Perez to the National Commission on Terrorist Attacks Upon the United States.

11. Ibid.

12. Ibid.

13. Ibid.

14. "Substitution for the Testimony of Mohammad Manea Ahmad al-Qahtani," *United States v. Zacarias Moussaoui* (No. 01-455), www.vaed.uscourts.gov/notablecases/moussaoui/exhibits/defense/944.pdf.

15. "Substitution for the Testimony of Khalid Sheikh Mohammed." *United States versus Zacarias Moussaoui* (No. 01-455-A), www.vaed.uscourts.gov/notablecases/moussaoui/exhibits/defense/941.pdf.

16. Statement of Jose E. Melendez-Perez to the National Commission on Terrorist Attacks Upon the United States.

17. Jose Melendez-Perez, interview by Michael Smerconish.

18. Statement of Jose E. Melendez-Perez to the National Commission on Terrorist Attacks Upon the United States.

19. Ibid.

20. Ibid.

21. Ibid.

22. Ibid.

23. Ibid.

24. Jose Melendez-Perez, interview by Michael Smerconish.

25. Statement of Jose E. Melendez-Perez to the National Commission on Terrorist Attacks Upon the United States.

26. Ibid.

27. Jose Melendez-Perez, interview by Michael Smerconish.

28. Ibid.

29. Ibid.

30. Statement of Jose E. Melendez-Perez to the National Commission on Terrorist Attacks Upon the United States.

31. Ibid.

32. Ibid.

33. Ibid.

34. Ibid.

35. Ibid.

36. Ibid.

37. "Substitution for the Testimony of Khalid Sheikh Mohammed," *United States vs. Zacarias Moussaoui.*

38. Jose Melendez-Perez, interview by Michael Smerconish.

39. Ibid.

40. Ibid.

41. Ibid.

42. Ibid.

43. Ibid.

44. Ibid.

Chapter Four

1. Malcolm Gladwell, "What is *Blink* about?" www .gladwell.com/blink/.

2. Ibid.

3. Diana Dean, interview by Michael Smerconish, February 10, 2007.

4. Colin Nickerson, "In Canada, terrorists found a haven," *Boston Globe*, April 9, 2001, www.highbeam.com/ doc/1P2-8645799.html.

5. Diana Dean, interview by Michael Smerconish.

6. Bruce Schneier, "Profile: Hinky," *Boston Globe*, November 24, 2004, www.boston.com/news/globe/ editorial_opinion/oped/articles/2004/11/24/ profile_hinky/.

7. Lisa Myers, "Foiling millennium attack was mostly luck." NBC News, April 29, 2004. www.msnbc.msn.com/ id/4864792/from/ET/.

8. Murray Weiss, "Flashy fed foresaw bin Laden's terror," *New York Post*, August 10, 2003.

9. Diana Dean, interview by Michael Smerconish.

10. Ibid.

11. Ibid.

12. Hal Bernton, Mike Carter, David Heath, and James Neff, "The terrorist within: The story behind one man's holy war against America," *Seattle Times*, June 23–July 7, 2002, http://seattletimes.nwsource.com/news/nation-world/terroristwithin.

13. Ibid.

14. Ibid.

15. Diana Dean, interview by Michael Smerconish.

16. Ibid.

17. Ibid.

18. Ibid.

19. Ibid.

20. "Prepared Statement by Diana Dean, United States Customs Inspector," U.S. Senate Judiciary Committee, 106th Congress (Second Session), February 10, 2000, www.gpo.gov/fdsys/pkg/CHRG-106shrg1063/html/CHRG-106shrg1063.htm.

21. Diana Dean, interview by Michael Smerconish.

22. Ibid.

23. Ibid.

24. Ibid.

25. Ibid.

26. Ibid.

27. Ibid.

28. Colin Nickerson, "In Canada, terrorists found a haven," *Boston Globe*, April 9, 2001, www.highbeam.com/doc/1P2-8645799.html.

29. Ibid.

30. Ibid.

31. Ibid.

32. Ibid.

33. Peter Urban, "2001 alert may have helped," *Connecticut Post*, April 11, 2004.

34. Diana Dean, interview by Michael Smerconish.

35. Ibid.

36. Lisa Myers, "Foiling millennium attack was mostly luck." NBC News, April 29, 2004, www.msnbc.msn.com/id/4864792/from/ET/.

37. Elaine Kamarck, "Best defense against terror is the cop on the beat," *Newsday*, July 22, 2005, http://belfercenter.ksg.harvard.edu/publication/1447/best_defense_against_terror_is_the_cop_on_the_beat.html.

38. Mike Carter, "Millenium bomber changes story about friend," *Seattle Times*, January 4, 2007, http://seattletimes.nwsource.com/html/localnews/2003508560_ressamletter04m.html; Jill Preschel, "22 years for millennium bomb plot," Associated Press, July 27, 2005, www.cbsnews.com/stories/2005/07/27/national/main712240.shtml.

39. Jane Fritsch, "Algerian sentenced in 1999 plot to bomb airport," *New York Times*, January 17, 2002, http://select.nytimes.com/gst/abstract.html?res=F70D13F83A5C0C748DDDA80894DA404482&n=Top%2fReference%2fTimes%20Topics%2fPeople%2fH%2fHaouari%2c%20Mokhtar.

40. Benjamin Weiser, "Conviction Upheld in Bomb Plot," *New York Times*, January 28, 2003, http://query.nytimes.com/gst/fullpage.html?res=9E02E7D61339F93BA15752C0A9659C8B63&n=Top%2fReference%2fTimes%20Topics%2fPeople%2fH%2fHaouari%2c%20Mokhtar.

41. Mike Carter, "Millenium bomber changes story about friend," *Seattle Times*, January 4, 2007, http://seattletimes.nwsource.com/html/localnews/2003508560_ressam letter04m.html

42. Ibid.

43. Letter from Rassam Ahmed to Judge Coughinour, November 11, 2006, http://seattletimes.nwsource.com/ABPub/2007/01/03/2003508150.pdf.

44. Ibid.

45. Melinda Hennenberger, "Terror in Oklahoma: The trooper, a by-the-book officer, 'suspicious by nature,' spots trouble and acts fast," *New York Times*, April 23, 1995, www.nytimes.com/1995/04/23/us/terror-oklahoma-trooper-book-officer-suspicious-nature-spots-trouble-acts-fast.html.

46. Jo Thomas, "Trial begins in the Oklahoma City bombing case," *New York Times*, April 25, 1997, www.nytimes.com/1997/04/25/us/trial-begins-in-the-oklahoma-city-bombing-case.html?scp=5&sq=Ryder%20truck%20day%20care&st=cse&pagewanted=1.

47. John Kifner, "Ten years after bombing, Oklahoma City remembers," *New York Times*, April 20, 2005, www.nytimes.com/2005/04/20/national/20oklahoma.html?_r=1&scp=3&sq=Oklahoma%20City%20Bombing%2019%20children&st=cse.

48. "McVeigh Remorseless About Bombing," Associated Press, March 29, 2001, http://www.rickross.com/reference/mcveigh/mcveigh6.html.

49. Al Baker, "Bust may be tied to Okla. Blast," *New York Daily News*, May 15, 1995, www.nydailynews.com/archives/news/1995/05/13/1995-05-13_bust_may_be_tied_to_okla__bl.html.

50. Kim Morava, "Trooper who arrested Timothy McVeigh shares story," *Shawnee News-Star*, February 24, 2009, www.news-star.com/archive/x844642367/Trooper-who-arrested-Timothy-McVeigh-shares-story.

51. Melinda Hennenberger, "Terror in Oklahoma, *New York Times*, April 23, 1995.

52." 'Turner Diaries' introduced in McVeigh trial," CNN .com, April 28, 1997, www.cnn.com/US/9704/28/okc/

53. Ibid.

54. Ibid.

55. Melinda Hennenberger, "Terror in Oklahoma, *New York Times*, April 23, 1995.

56. Ibid.

57. John Kifner, "Terror in Oklahoma: The Suspect; Authorities hold a man of 'extreme right wing views,'" *New York Times*, April 22, 1995, www.nytimes.com/1995/04/22/us/terror-oklahoma-suspect-authorities-hold-man-extreme-right-wing-views.html?scp=1&sq=McVeigh%20almost%20released%20on%20bail&st=cse.

58. Melinda Hennenberger, "Terror in Oklahoma, *New York Times*, April 23, 1995.

59. "McVeigh Remorseless About Bombing." Associated Press, March 29, 2001.

60. "Timothy McVeigh: Convicted Oklahoma City bomber," CNN, March 29, 2001, http://archives.cnn .com/2001/US/03/29/profile.mcveigh/.

61. "Hero captor to ignore his prisoner's demise," *New York Post*, June 10, 2001.

62. "Officer of the Month, October 2001: Second Lieutenant Charles Hanger," National Law Enforcement Officers' Memorial Fund, www.nleomf.com/TheFund/programs/OOM/hanger_oct01.htm.

63. Ibid.

64. Ibid.

65. "Text of the Moussaoui e-mail," CNN.com, February 8, 2002, http://edition.cnn.com/2002/US/02/08/inv .moussaoui.email.text/.

66. "Timeline: The case against Zacarias Moussaoui," NPR.org, May 3, 2006, www.npr.org/templates/story/ story.php?storyId=5243788.

67. John Cloud, "Atta's Odyssey," *Time*, September 30, 2001, www.time.com/time/magazine/article/ 0,9171,176917-1,00.html.

68. "Text of the Moussaoui e-mail." CNN, February 8, 2002.

69. Daniel Pipes, "Zacarias Moussaoui Asked: Can an Airplane Pilot Shut off Oxygen to the Passengers?" *Front Page Magazine*, April 29, 2005, www.danielpipes.org/ article/2564.

70. Suzanne Daley, "A nation challenged: The suspect: Mysterious life of a subject from France," *New York Times*, September 21, 2001, www.nytimes.com/2001/09/21/ world/a-nation-challenged-the-suspect-mysterious-life-of- a-suspect-from-france.html.

71. Bruce Crumley, "High-Alert Holidays," *Time Magazine*, December 14, 2003, www.time.com/time/magazine/ article/0,9171,561279,00.html; Jack Kelley, "Malaysia site of Sept. 11 plotting, FBI report says." *USA Today*, January 30, 2002, www.usatoday.com/news/sept11/2002/01/29/usat- malaysia.htm.

72. Phil Hirschkorn, "Moussaoui was a flight school washout," CNN.com, March 9, 2006, www.cnn.com/2006/ LAW/03/09/moussaoui.trial/.

73. "U.S. refuses to let Moussaoui call witness," CNN .com, July 15, 2003, www.cnn.com/2003/LAW/07/14/ moussaoui/.

74. "Transcript: U.S. Army launches criminal investigation into Pat Tillman's death; Bush returns from trip to South Asia," CNN.com, March 5, 2006, http://edition.cnn.hu/TRANSCRIPTS/0603/05/sm.01.html; Greg Gordon, "How 2 men helped FBI bring down Moussaoui," *Minneapolis Star Tribune*, April 24, 2005, www.highbeam.com/doc/1G1-131910170.html.

75. Ibid.

76. Ibid.

77. Ibid.

78. Ibid.

79. Ibid.

80. Ibid.

81. Ibid.

82. Ibid.

83. Ibid.

84. Ibid.

85. *United States of America v. Zacarias Moussaoui*. Indictment. www.usdoj.gov/ag/moussaouiindictment.htm.

86. Daniel Pipes, "Zacarias Moussaoui Asked," *Front Page*, April 29, 2005.

87. Greg Gordon, "Senate honors 2 men."

88. Greg Gordon, "How 2 men helped FBI."

89. Greg Gordon, "Senate honors 2 men."

90. Greg Gordon, "How 2 men helped FBI."

91. Richard A. Serrano, "Moussaoui says he was to fly fifth plane," *Los Angeles Times*, March 28, 2006, http://articles.latimes.com/2006/mar/28/nation/na-moussa28.

92. Matthew Barakat, "Moussaoui testifies he was to fly 5th plane into White House in 9/11 plot," Associated Press, March 27, 2006, www.signonsandiego.com/news/nation/terror/20060327-1349-moussaoui.html.

93. Richard Serrano, "Moussaoui says he was to fly fifth plane."

94. Ibid.

95. Daniel Strieff, "Terror-tinged UK mosque gets a make-over," MSNBC.com, July 5, 2006, www.msnbc.msn.com/id/13501930/.

96. "Moussaoui praises bin Laden, says case against him based on false theory," Associated Press, July 2, 2002, www.foxnews.com/story/0,2933,56753,00.html.

97. "Fast Facts: Quotes from Moussaoui," FoxNews.com, March 27, 2006, www.foxnews.com/story/0,2933,189262,00.html

98. Charlie Savage, "Moussaoui now says White House was his attack target on Sept. 11," *Boston Globe*, March 28, 2006, www.boston.com/news/nation/washington/articles/2006/03/28/moussaoui_now_says_white_house_was_his_attack_target_on_sept_11/.

99. Jerry Markon and Timothy Dwyer, "Moussaoui says he was to fly 5th plane; White House attack planned for 9/11, terrorist testifies," *Washington Post*, March 28, 2006, www.michigandaily.com/content/moussaoui-says-he-was-fly-5th-plane-911.

100. "Al-Qaida plotters dismiss Moussaoui's role," Associated Press, March 28, 2006, http://ads.omaha.com/media/maps/cws2005/www.omaha.com/indexab29.html?u_pg=2323&u_sid=100109861; William Glaberson, "5 charged in 9/11 attacks seek to plead guilty," *New York Times*, December 8, 2008, www.nytimes.com/2008/12/09/us/09gitmo.html?_r=1&pagewanted=all.

101. "Al-Qaida plotters dismiss Moussaoui's role." Associated Press, March 28, 2006.

102. Ibid.

103. Jerry Markon and Timothy Dwyer, "Horror takes the stand at the Moussaoui trial," *Washington Post*, April 2006, www.washingtonpost.com/wp-dyn/content/article/2006/04/06/AR2006040600818.html.

104. Ibid.

105. Ibid.

106. Ibid.

107. Ibid.

108. Marc Santora, "Some 9/11 families side with jury on Moussaoui, but most express regrets," *New York Times*, May 4, 2006, http://query.nytimes.com/gst/fullpage.html?res=9F03E0DA1E3FF937A35756C0A9609C8B63&sec=&spon=.

109. Steve Sailer, "Malcolm Gladwell's *Blinks* at Racial Realities," January 30, 2005, www.vdare.com/sailer/050130_blink.htm.

110. Malcolm Gladwell, "The New-Boy Network," *New Yorker*, May 29, 2000, www.gladwell.com/2000/2000_05_29_a_interview.htm.

111. Ibid.

112. Judge Richard A. Posner, "Blinkered," *New Republic*, January 24, 2005, http://www.cs.ucl.ac.uk/staff/d.quercia/others/blinkered.html.

113. Michael Smerconish, "He looked terror in the eye—and blinked," *Philadelphia Daily News*, February 24, 2005, www.mastalk.com/daily_news2/02_24_2005.htm.

114. Ibid.

115. Ibid.

116. Ibid.

117. Ibid.

118. Ibid.

119. Ibid.

120. Ibid.

Chapter Five

1. National Commission on Terrorist Attacks Upon the United States, *Final Report of the National Commission on Terrorist Attacks Upon the United States*, 10, http://govinfo .library.unt.edu/911/report/911Report.pdf.

2. Ibid., 8.

3. Ibid.

4. Information provided by the Flight 93 National Memorial.

5. Ibid.

6. *Final Report of the National Commission on Terrorist Attacks Upon the United States*, 10.

7. Ibid., 8.

8. Ibid., 10.

9. Ibid.

10. Ibid. 12.

11. Flight 93 National Memorial.

12. *United States v. Zacarias Moussaoui*, Prosecution Trial Exhibit No. P200055, www.vaed.uscourts.gov/notable cases/moussaoui/exhibits/prosecution/flights/P200055 .html.

13. "Hero's last words are immortalized by his wife," *Oakland Tribune*, September 11, 2003, http://findarticles .com/p/articles/mi_qn4176/is_20030911/ai_n14554712/.

14. "Linda Gronlund recorded call to sister," FBI, unclassified, January 26, 2007.

15. *Final Report of the National Commission on Terrorist Attacks Upon the United States*, 10.

16. Lisa Jefferson, *Called: Hello, My Name Is Mrs. Jefferson. I Understand Your Plane is Being Hijacked*, (Northfield Publishers, 2006); Lisa Beamer, *Let's Roll* (Tindale House Publishers, 2002).

17. "Text of Flight 93 Recording," Associated Press, April 12, 2006, www.foxnews.com/story/0,2933,191520,00.html.

18. Jerry Markon and Timothy Dwyer, "At trial, Flight 93 Myth Finally Becomes Reality," *Washington Post*, April 13, 2006, www.mail-archive.com/osint@yahoogroups.com/msg20454.html.

19. Ibid.

20. Ibid.

21. Edward Felt call to Westmoreland County 9-1-1 Center. Source: FBI, unclassified January 26, 2007.

22. Information provided by the Flight 93 National Memorial.

23. *Final Report of the National Commission on Terrorist Attacks Upon the United States*, 30.

24. Flight 93 National Memorial.

25. Sara Rimer and Jere Longman, "Searchers find plane cockpit voice recorder," *New York Times*, September 15, 2001, www.nytimes.com/2001/09/15/us/after-attacks-pennsylvania-crash-searchers-find-plane-cockpit-voice-recorder.html.

26. "FBI completes Flight 93 investigation," The Pittsburgh Channel, September 24, 2001, www.thepittsburghchannel.com/news/970609/detail.html.

27. Flight 93 National Memorial.

Chapter Six

1. National Commission on Terrorist Attacks Upon the United State, *Final Report of the National Commission on Terrorist Attacks Upon the United States*, 385, http://govinfo.library.unt.edu/911/report/911Report.pdf.

2. R.W. Apple, "After the Attacks: Assessment; President seems to gain legitimacy," *New York Times*, September

16, 2001, www.nytimes.com/2001/09/16/us/after-the-attacks-assessment-president-seems-to-gain-legitimacy.html?scp=2&sq=George%20W.%20Bush&pagewanted=all.

3. *Final Report of the National Commission on Terrorist Attacks Upon the United States*, 385.

4. Ibid., 387.

5. Ibid.

6. Ibid.

7. Commissioner Robert C. Bonner, interview by Michael Smerconish, February 5, 2007.

8. Ibid.

9. Ibid.

10. Ibid.

11. Assistant Commissioner Jayson P. Ahern, interview by Michael Smerconish, February 6, 2007.

12. Robert C. Bonner, interview by Michael Smerconish.

13. Ibid.

14. Ibid.

15. Ibid.

16. Ibid.

17. Ibid.

18. Daniel Pipes, "The California Suicide Bomber: Ra'ed Mansour al-Banna," *Front Page Magazine*, April 4, 2005, www.danielpipes.org/article/2497.

19. Robert C. Bonner, interview by Michael Smerconish.

20. Daniel Pipes, "The California Suicide Bomber, *Front Page Magazine*.

21. Shadi Rahimi, "U.S. entry increasingly being denied," *St. Petersburg Times*, April 21, 2006, www.sptimes.com/2006/04/21/Worldandnation/US_entry_increasingly.shtml.

22. Robert C. Bonner, interview by Michael Smerconish.

23. United States Department of Homeland Security, "U.S. Customs Names Ahern Assistant Commissioner of Field Operations," press release, June 21, 2002, www.cbp .gov/xp/cgov/newsroom/news_releases/archives/ legacy/2002/62002/06212002.xml.

24. Jayson P. Ahern, interview by Michael Smerconish.

25. Ibid.

26. Ibid.

27. Ibid.

28. Barry McManus, interview by Michael Smerconish, February 7, 2007.

29. Ibid.

30. Ibid.

31. Ibid.

32. Ibid.

33. Ibid.

34. Ibid.

35. Ibid.

36. Ibid.

37. Thomas Frank, "Suspects' body language can blow their cover," *USA Today*, December 27, 2005, www.usa today.com/news/nation/2005-12-27-body-language_x .htm?csp=34.

38. Ibid.

39. Ibid.

40. Jane Engle, "TSA screeners being trained to monitor people, not just bags," *Los Angeles Times*, August 27, 2006, http://travel.latimes.com/articles/la-tr-insider27aug27.

41. Ibid.

42. Ibid.

43. Thomas Frank, "Suspects' body language can blow their cover."

44. Ibid.

45. Ibid.

46. Thomas Frank, "Airport security uses talk as tactic." *USA Today*, December 28, 2005, www.usatoday.com/travel/news/2005-12-28-airport-security_x.htm.

47. Ibid.

48. Ibid.

49. Ibid.

50. Sally B. Donnell, "A New Tack for Airport Screening: Behave Yourself," *Time*, May 17, 2006, www.time.com/time/nation/article/0,8599,1195330,00.html.

51. Ibid.

52. Allison Hanley, "Fighting weapons of mass effect," *CBP Today*, December/January 2007, www.cbp.gov/xp/CustomsToday/2007/dec_jan/fighting_weapons.xml.

53. Ibid.

54. Ibid.

55. Ian Sample, "The brain scan that can read people's intentions," *The Guardian*, February 9, 2007, www.guardian.co.uk/science/2007/feb/09/neuroscience.ethicsofscience.

56. Ibid.

57. Ibid.

58. Ibid.

59. Ibid.

60. Ian Sample, "Honda unveils helmet that lets wearer control a robot by thought alone," *The Guardian*, March 31, 2009, www.guardian.co.uk/science/2009/mar/31/mind-control-helmet-honda-asimo.

61. Michael Matza, "Software used to predict who might kill," *Philadelphia Inquirer*, December 3, 2006, www.highbeam.com/doc/1G1-155367298.html.

62. Ibid.

63. Shaun Waterman, "Dems slam border screening rules." UPI, January 2, 2007, www.spacedaily.com/reports/Dems_Slam_Border_Screening_Rules_999.html.

64. Ibid.

65. Ibid.

66. Thomas Frank, "Airport uses talk as tactic," *USA Today*, December 28, 2006, www.usatoday.com/news/nation/2005-12-28-airport-security_x.htm.

67. Ibid.

68. Thomas Frank, "Suspects' body language can blow their cover," *USA Today*, December 27, 2005, www.usatoday.com/news/nation/2005-12-27-body-language_x.htm?csp=34.

69. Ibid.

70. *Final Report of the National Commission on Terrorist Attacks Upon the United States*, 384.

71. *9/11 and Terrorist Travel: Staff Report of the National Commission on Terrorist Attacks Upon the United States*, 2004, 164, www.9-11commission.gov/staff_statements/911_Terr Trav_Monograph.pdf.

72. *Final Report of the National Commission on Terrorist Attacks Upon the United States*, 389.

73. Brian Goebel, interview by Michael Smerconish. *The Michael Smerconish Show*, WPHT 1210 AM, Philadelphia, December 12, 2006.

74. Ibid.

75. Ibid.

76. Ibid.

77. Ibid.

78. Ibid.

79. Ibid.

80. Ibid.

81. Ibid.

82. Ibid.

83. Ginger Thompson, "New requirements on border I.D. stir worry at crossings," *New York Times*, May 23, 2009, www.nytimes.com/2009/05/24/world/americas/24border .html?ref=business.

84. Leslie Berestein, "New rites of passage debut," *San Diego Union-Tribune*, June 2, 2009, www3.signonsandiego .com/stories/2009/jun/02/new-rites-passage-debut/.

85. Malcolm Gladwell, "The New-Boy Network," *New Yorker*, May 29, 2000, www.gladwell.com/ 2000/2000_05_29_a_interview.htm.

Chapter Seven

1. Senate Committee on Armed Services, *Inquiry into the Treatment of Detainees in U.S. Custody*, 110th Congress, 2d session, November 20, 2008 (released April 22, 2009), http://armed-services.senate.gov/Publications/ Detainee%20Report%20Final_April%2022%202009.pdf.

2. Tim Golden and Don Van Natta Jr., "The Reach of War; U.S. said to overstate value of Guantanamo detainees," *New York Times*, June 21, 2004, www.nytimes.com/2004/06/21/ world/the-reach-of-war-us-said-to-overstate-value-of-guantanamo-detainees.html?pagewanted=all.

3. United States Department of Defense, "Guantanamo Provides Valuable Intelligence Information," U.S. Department of Defense, press release, June 12, 2005, www .defenselink.mil/releases/2005/nr20050612-3661.html.

4. Tim Golden and Don Van Natta Jr., "The Reach of War; U.S. said to overstate value of Guantanamo detainees."

5. Senate Committee on Armed Services, *Inquiry into the Treatment of Detainees in U.S. Custody.*

6. Ibid.

7. "FBI letter complains of aggressive interrogation at Guantanamo in 2002," Associated Press, December 6, 2004, www.usatoday.com/news/world/2004-12-06-gitmo-fbi-abuse_x.htm.

8. T.J. Harrington, deputy assistant director, Terrorism Division. U.S. Department of Justice, to Major General Donald J. Ryder, July 14, 2004, http://humanrights.ucdavis .edu/resources/fbi-documents/FBI87_001914%20to%20 001916_DOJFBI001914.pdf.

9. Senate Committee on Armed Services, *Inquiry into the Treatment of Detainees in U.S. Custody.*

10. Ibid.

11. Ibid.

12. Ibid.

13. Ibid.

14. Ibid.

15. Ibid.

16. Ibid.

17. Ibid.

18. Ibid.

19. Ibid.

20. Ibid.

21. Adam Zagorin, "Detainee 063: A Broken Man?" *Time*, March 2, 2006, www.time.com/time/nation/ article/0,8599,1169310,00.html.

22. Adam Zagorin and Michael Duff, "Inside the Interrogation of Detainee 063," *Time*, June 20, 2005, www.time .com/time/magazine/article/0,9171,1071284,00.html.

23. "Interrogation Log: Detainee 063." Published in *Time*, March 2, 2006, www.time.com/time/2006/log/log.pdf.

24. Ibid.

25. Ibid.

26. Ibid.

27. Ibid.

28. Ibid.

29. Ibid.

30. Ibid.

31. Ibid.

32. Ibid.

33. Ibid.

34. Ibid.

35. Ibid.

36. Ibid.

37. Ibid.

38. Ibid.

39. Ibid.

40. Ibid.

41. Ibid.

42. Ibid.

43. Ibid.

44. Senate Committee on Armed Services, *Inquiry into the Treatment of Detainees in U.S. Custody.*

45. Drew Brown, "Coercive methods prompted Sept. 11 figure to talk, general testifies," Knight Ridder Newspapers, July 13, 2005, www.mcclatchydc.com/190/story/12102.html.

46. Adam Zagorin, " '20th Hijacker' says torture made him lie," *Time*, March 3, 2006, www.time.com/time/nation/article/0,8599,1169322,00.html.

47. Drew Brown, "Coercive methods prompted Sept. 11 figure to talk, general testifies."

48. Ibid.

49. United States Department of Defense, "Guantanamo Provides Valuable Intelligence Information," press release, June 12, 2005, www.defenselink.mil/releases/2005/ nr20050612-3661.html.

50. Ibid.

51. Ibid.

52. John Yoo, interview by Michael Smerconish, *The Michael Smerconish Program*, 1210 WPHT AM, Philadelphia, November 14, 2006.

53. Ibid.

54. Adam Zagorin. "Detainee 063: A Broken Man?"

55. Joby Warrick and Julie Tate, "Report calls CIA detainee treatment 'inhuman,'" *Washington Post*, April 7, 2009, www.washingtonpost.com/wp-dyn/content/ article/2009/04/06/AR2009040603654.html.

56. International Committee of the Red Cross, "ICRC Report on the Treatment of Fourteen 'High Value Detainees' in CIA Custody," February 2007, www.nybooks.com/ icrc-report.pdf.

57. Adam Zagorin. "Detainee 063: A Broken Man?"

58. Office for the Administrative Review of Enemy Combatants at U.S. Naval Base, Guantanamo Bay, Cuba, United States Department of Defense, "Summary of Evidence for Combatant Status Review Tribunal—Al Qahtani, Muhammad Mani Ahmed Al Shai Lan," October 21, 2004, http://projects.nytimes.com/guantanamo/detainees/63- mohammed-al-qahtani.

59. Ibid.

60. Office for the Administrative Review of Enemy Combatants at U.S. Naval Base, Guantanamo Bay, Cuba, United States Department of Defense, "Unclassified Summary of Evidence for Administrative Review Board in the Case of Al Qahtani, Muhammad Mani Ahmed Al Shal Lan," October 31, 2005, http://projects.nytimes.com/guantanamo/detainees/63-mohammed-al-qahtani/documents/1/pages/91.

61. Ibid.

62. Ibid.

63. Ibid.

64. Ibid.

65. Ibid.

66. Ibid.

67. Office for the Administrative Review of Enemy Combatants at U.S. Naval Base, Guantanamo Bay, Cuba, United States Department of Defense, "Summary of Administrative Review Board Proceedings for ISN 063, 2006, http://projects.nytimes.com/guantanamo/detainees/63-mohammed-al-qahtani/documents/6/pages/30.

68. Ibid.

69. Ibid.

70. Ibid.

71. Ibid.

72. Ibid.

73. Ibid.

74. Ibid.

75. Ibid.

76. Ibid.

77. Ibid.

78. Ibid.

79. Ibid.

80. Ibid.

81. Office for the Administrative Review of Enemy Combatants at U.S. Naval Base, Guantanamo Bay, Cuba, United States Department of Defense, "Unclassified Summary of Evidence for Administrative Review Board in the Case of Al Qahtani, Maad," January 17, 2008, http://projects.nytimes.com/guantanamo/detainees/63-mohammed-al-qahtani/documents/3/pages/127#7.

82. Ibid.

83. Ibid.

84. Ibid.

85. Ibid.

86. Ibid.

87. Adam Zagorin and Michael Duffy, "Inside the Interrogation of Detainee 063," *Time*, June 20, 2005, www.time.com/time/magazine/article/0,9171,1071284,00.html.

88. "Substitution for the testimony of Khalid Sheikh Mohammed," *United States vs. Zacarias Moussaoui* (No. 01-455-A), www.vaed.uscourts.gov/notablecases/moussaoui/exhibits/defense/941.pdf.

89. Ibid.

90. Ibid.

91. Ibid.

92. Ibid.

93. "Terrorism 101: A How-To Guide" [The Manchester Document], The Smoking Gun (Web site), www.thesmokinggun.com/archive/jihadmanual.html.

94. Donna Miles, "Al Qaeda Manual Drives Detainee Behavior at Guantanamo Bay." Armed Forces Press Service, June 29, 2005, www.defenselink.mil/news/newsarticle.aspx?id=16270.

95. "Terrorism 101: A How-To Guide" [The Manchester Document]. The Smoking Gun, www.thesmokinggun.com/archive/jihadmanual.html. Accessed May 25, 2009.

96. Ibid.

97. "Charges dropped against '20th' hijacker," Associated Press, May 12, 2008, www.msnbc.msn.com/id/24587062/.

98. Bob Woodward, "Detainee tortured, says U.S. official," *Washington Post*, January 14, 2009, www.washingtonpost.com/wp-dyn/content/article/2009/01/13/AR2009011303372.html.

99. Ibid.

101. William Glaberson, "Detainee was tortured, a Bush official confirms," *New York Times*, January 14, 2009, www.nytimes.com/2009/01/14/us/14gitmo.html?_r=1.

102. Bob Woodward, "Detainee tortured, says U.S. official."

103. Ibid.

104. Ibid.

105. Mark Mazzetti and Scott Shane, "Interrogation memos detail harsh tactics by the C.I.A," *New York Times*, April 10, 2009, www.nytimes.com/2009/04/17/us/politics/17detain.html?hp.

106. Ibid.

107. Ibid.

108. Ibid.

109. "The Torturers' Manifestor," editorial, *New York Times*, April 18, 2009, www.nytimes.com/2009/04/19/opinion/19sun1.html?_r=1&ref=opinion.

110. "Close the torture loophole," *Los Angeles Times*, April 18, 2009, www.latimes.com/news/opinion/editorials/la-ed-torture18-2009apr18,0,5961666.story.

111. "Dealing with a Disgrace," editorial, *Washington Post*, April 17, 2009, www.washingtonpost.com/wp-dyn/content/article/2009/04/16/AR2009041603911.html.

112. Michael Hayden and Michael Mukasey, "The President ties his own hands on terror," *Wall Street Journal*, April 17, 2009, http://online.wsj.com/article/SB123993446103128041.html.

113. Ibid.

114. Peter Finn and Joby Warrick, "Detainee's harsh treatment foiled no plots," *Washington Post*, March 29, 2009, http:// washingtonpost.com/wp-dyn/content/article/2009/03/28/AR2009032802066_pf.html.

115. Ibid.

116. Ibid.

117. Ibid.

118. Ibid.

Epilogue

1. Transcript, *Scarborough Country*, April 12, 2006, http://msnbc.msn.com/id/12301552/.

2. Flight 93 National Memorial, "Temporary Memorial," www.honorflight93.org/memorial/temporary-memorial.cfm.

3. Pennsylvania Governor Mark Schweiker, e-mail interview by Michael Smerconish, November 14, 2005.

4. Flight 93 National Memorial, "The Story," www.honorflight93.org/story/.

5. Steve Goldstein, "Memorial to Flight 93 finalized; 'The Crescent of Embrace' will honor the passengers and crew who died in Shanksville, Pa., on 9/11. It's a place to heal,'" *Philadelphia Inquirer*, September 8, 2005.

6. Michael A. Smerconish, "Postcard From Shanksville," *Philadelphia Daily News*, September 29 2005, www .mastalk.com/daily_news2/09_29_2005.htm.

7. Ibid.

8. Ibid.

9. Adam Dawtrey and Gabriel Snyder, " 'United' states case: Biz keeps eye on '93,' " April 24, 2006, www.variety .com/article/VR1117942006.html?categoryid=10&cs=1.

10. "United Airlines Flight #93 Cockpit Voice Recorder Transcript," *United States v. Zacarias Moussaoui* (No. 01-455), www.thesmokinggun.com/archive/ 0412061hijack1.html.

11. Neil A. Lewis, "Final Struggles on 9/11 Plane Fill Courtroom," *New York Times*, April 13, 2006, www.nytimes.com/2006/04/13/us/13moussaoui .html?pagewanted=print

12. "United Airlines Flight #93 Cockpit Voice Recorder Transcript." 455.

13. Karen Breslau, "The Final Moments of Flight 93," *Newsweek*, September 22, 2001, http://msnbc.msn.com/ id/3067652/.

14. Pennsylvania Governor Mark Schweiker, e-mail interview by Michael Smerconish, November 14, 2005.

15. National Park Service, "Pure Pilgrimage: More than one million people visit Flight 93 crash site in Shanksville, Pennsylvania," press release, April 21, 2009. www.nps.gov/ flni/parknews/upload/pure_pilgramage.pdf.

16. "Flight 93 National Memorial Mission Statement," National Park Service, www.nps.gov/flni/parkmgmt/ missionstatement.htm.

17. Sher Zieve, "Flight 93 National Memorial Project Responds," *National Ledger*, September 16, 2005,

www.nationalledger.com/cgi-bin/artman/exec/view
.cgi?archive=1&num=751

18. "The Memorial," Flight 93 National Memorial, www
.honorflight93.org/memorial/.

19. Staff of Flight 93 National Memorial Campaign,
phone conversation with Michael Smerconish, April, 2009.

20. Amy Worden, "U.S. gives Flight 93 site landowners
one week to sell," *Philadelphia Inquirer*, June 6, 2009, www
.philly.com/inquirer/local/pa/20090606_U_S__gives_
Flight_93_site_landowners_one_week_to_sell.html.

21. National Park Service, "Pure Pilgrimage."

22. "Flight 93 National Memorial Mission Statement,"
National Park Service.

INDEX

ABOUT THE AUTHOR

Michael A. Smerconish, attorney-turned-political commentator, has been recognized by *Talkers* magazine as one of America's most important talk show hosts. Named *Radio and Records'* Local Personality of the Year in 2009, Smerconish  now hosts two nationally syndicated daily radio programs, including a morning drive show based at Philadelphia's The Big Talker 1210 AM WPHT. Both programs are syndicated by Dial-Global in a partnership with CBS RADIO. He is the author of four books, including *Morning Drive* (Lyons Press), *Flying Blind*, and two *New York Times* bestsellers: *Murdered by Mumia* (Lyons Press) and *Muzzled: From T-Ball or Terrorism, True Stories That Should be Fiction*. Smerconish was a regular fill-in host for Bill O'Reilly's nationally syndicated *The Radio Factor* and has been a guest host on MSNBC's *Hardball with Chris Matthews*. He has appeared on every major television program where politics are discussed—from the *Colbert Report* to *The View*—and is a regular contributor at MSNBC. He also authors separate weekly columns for the *Philadelphia Daily News* and *Philadelphia Inquirer*. He lives in Montgomery County, Pennsylvania, with his wife and their four children.